CICERO AND THE END
OF THE ROMAN REPUBLIC

Current and forthcoming titles in the Classical World Series

Aristophanes and his Theatre of the Absurd, P. Cartledge
Athens and Sparta, S. Todd
Athens under the Tyrants, J. Smith
Attic Orators, M. Edwards
Augustan Rome, A. Wallace-Hadrill
Cicero and the End of the Roman Republic, T. Wiedemann
Classical Epic: Homer and Virgil, R. Jenkyns
Greece and the Persians, J. Sharwood Smith
Greek Architecture, R. Tomlinson
Greek Tragedy: An Introduction, M. Baldock
Julio-Claudian Emperors, T. Wiedemann
Morals and Values in Ancient Greece, J. Ferguson
Religion and the Greeks, R. Garland
Religion and the Romans, K. Dowden
Roman Architecture, Martin Thorpe
Roman Britain, S.J. Hill and S. Ireland
Roman Satirists, S. Braund
Slavery in Classical Greece, N. Fisher

Classical World series

CICERO AND THE END
OF THE ROMAN REPUBLIC

Thomas Wiedemann

Bristol Classical Press

General Editor: John H. Betts
Series Editor: Michael Gunningham

First published in 1994 by
Bristol Classical Press
an imprint of
Gerald Duckworth & Co. Ltd
The Old Piano Factory
48 Hoxton Square, London N1 6PB

Reprinted 1995

A catalogue record for this book is available
from the British Library

ISBN 1-85399-193-7

Available in USA and Canada from:
Focus Information Group
PO Box 369
Newburyport
MA 01950

Printed and bound by Antony Rowe Ltd, Eastbourne

Contents

Acknowledgements   vi

List of Illustrations   vii

Map of Italy   viii

Table of Dates   ix

Map of the Mediterranean   x

1. Militarism, Competitive Politics, and Empire   1

2. Competitiveness and the Creation of a Graeco-Roman Culture   7

3. New Men and Old Families   15

4. The Army in Politics   24

5. The Sullan Regime   29

6. Challenging Hortensius   33

7. To the Top of the Ladder   38

8. Cicero's Year   42

9. Exclusion and Exile   47

10. The Dynasts in Control   53

11. Cicero the *Imperator*   59

12. Cicero the Writer   64

13. Caesar and his Political Successors   71

14. *Philippics*   76

15. Failure and Success   82

Suggestions for Further Study   85

Suggestions for Further Reading   87

Some Technical Terms   91

Acknowledgements

Jonathan Powell, John Rich, and Niall Rudd read the draft version of this book with great care, pointing out errors of fact and of English, and warning me against explaining Cicero's literary achievement too cynically as a function of political competition. I am very grateful to them for their help. In spite of their reservations, I have resisted the tendency – all too frequent in biographies – to heroise Cicero. There is also a tendency to represent the magnates of the Roman republic as more moral than those of the empire, perhaps because we are brought up to see the republic as more like the pluralist parliamentary system through which we ourselves are governed. Cicero and his contemporaries may not have had the untrammelled power of the later emperors, but that did not make them any less devious and self-interested. They all had blood on their hands. That does not of course detract from Cicero's cultural achievement: it is an old paradox that good can come from the worst of motives.

My thanks are also due to Michael Gunningham and the staff at BCP, and to Sue Grice for her illustrations and Christine Hall for her drawings of coins.

Where not otherwise stated, dates are BC. BC also stands for *Bellum Civile*, the title of Caesar's and Appian's accounts of the Roman civil wars; NH stands for *Naturalis Historia*, Pliny the Elder's encyclopaedia; and *Ad Att.* and *Ad Fam.* are the collections of Cicero's letters to Atticus and to his other correspondents.

For ease of reference, the titles of many of Cicero's works will be found in bold print at the point where I have tried to include a brief statement of the content of that particular work. English versions of these titles have been given only where the meaning is not immediately obvious from the Latin. The Latin titles are dispensed with where they are not usually used (e.g. for the *Verrines*).

This reprint incorporates several points raised by reviewers. I am particularly grateful to Robin Seager for suggesting various corrections and clarifications, especially on genealogical issues.

TEJW

List of Illustrations

Map of Italy viii

Map of the Mediterranean x

Fig. 1 Denarius with the symbol of the Metelli. [Drawing by 3
Christine Hall]

Fig. 2 Roman noble holding ancestral images ('Barberini statue'). 11

Fig. 3 Stemma of Cicero's family links. 14

Fig. 4 City gate at Arpinum. 17

Fig. 5 Denarius representing Marius' triumph. [Drawing by 18
Christine Hall]

Fig. 6 Denarius of the Italian confederacy. [Drawing by 22
Christine Hall]

Fig. 7 Marius. [Courtesy of Glyptothek, Munich] 26

Fig. 8 Stemma of the Sullan establishment. 28

Fig. 9 Denarius representing Rome and Italy. [Drawing by 30
Christine Hall]

Fig. 10 Sulla. [Courtesy of Glyptothek, Munich] 32

Fig. 11 Sarcophagus of Caecina Selcia. [Courtesy of Museo 39
Guarnacci, Volterra]

Fig. 12 Statue of an orator. [Courtesy of Soprintendenza 43
Archeologica, Florence]

Fig. 13 Denarius depicting voting at an assembly. [Drawing by 49
Christine Hall]

Fig. 14 Pompey. [Courtesy of Ny Carlsberg Glyptotek, 56
Copenhagen]

Fig. 15 Cistophorus of Apamea in Phrygia. [Drawing by 61
Christine Hall]

Fig. 16 Denarius of Caesar. 65

Fig. 17 Antony (Florence). 77

Fig. 18 Aureus of Brutus. 80

Fig. 19 The census of 70 BC (Louvre, Paris). [Drawing by 90
Sue Grice]

Map of Italy

Table of Dates

BC

133	Tribunate of Tiberius Gracchus.
123/22	Tribunate of Gaius Gracchus.
106	Cicero born, January 3rd.
91/89	Social War.
82	Battle of the Colline gate: Sulla seizes power.
80	*Pro Roscio Amerino.*
75	Cicero quaestor for western Sicily.
70	Crassus and Pompey consuls. *Verrines.*
66	Cicero praetor. Pompey replaces Lucullus in command of the campaign against Mithridates.
63	Cicero consul. Conspiracy of Catiline.
59	Caesar consul.
58	Tribunate of Clodius. Cicero flees Rome.
57	September: Cicero returns to Rome.
55	Second consulship of Crassus and Pompey.
53	Crassus killed at Carrhae.
52	Rioting between Clodius and Milo; death of Clodius; Pompey sole consul.
51/50	Cicero governor of Cilicia.
49	Caesar occupies Italy.
48	Pompey and the republicans defeated at Pharsalus.
44	Caesar assassinated on March 15th.
43	Cicero put to death, December 7th.
42	Brutus and Cassius defeated at Philippi.
31	Octavian defeats Antony at Actium; assumes control of the entire empire (as 'Augustus', from 27).
30	Cicero's son holds the consulship.

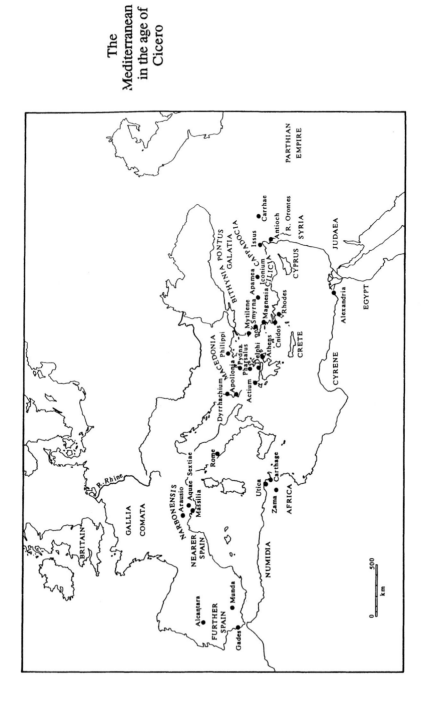

The
Mediterranean
in the age of
Cicero

Chapter 1
Militarism, Competitive Politics, and Empire

The values of the Roman republic into which Cicero was born were both militaristic and competitive. The political and military system which developed during the middle of the fourth century BC may in origin have been a defensive reaction to the dangers posed by other central Italian peoples. But because the system used warfare as a means of resolving rivalry between individuals and groups within Rome, it led inexorably first to Roman control over the rest of Latium (338), and then hegemony over the rest of Italy (Second Samnite War, 326-304; elimination of Etruscan opposition at the battle of Sentinum, 295; defeat of Pyrrhus and his South Italian allies, 282-272). Finally, the elimination of Carthage, the Seleucid empire, and Macedonia as major military powers at the battles of Zama (202), Magnesia (190), and Pydna (168) respectively, brought Roman domination of the entire Mediterranean world.

The principal military factor in this development, extraordinary not so much in the extent of its success, as in the fact that it could be sustained over many generations, was the legion. Its relatively open order made it a much more effective fighting force in the hill-countries of the Mediterranean littoral than the phalanxes of heavily-armed citizen-soldiers or mercenaries characteristic of the classical and Hellenistic periods. The effectiveness of the Roman army was enhanced by an internal political pluralism which combined competition within the élite for magistracies of short duration (thus preventing the emergence of excessively powerful individuals) with mechanisms allowing expression to be given to the concerns of interest-groups and individuals who did not hold office (through the assemblies and the plebeian tribunes). The need to find both military manpower and competent officers persuaded the 'patrician' clans (*gentes*) who had exercised control over public life since the overthrow of the monarchy (trad. 509 BC) to widen the circle of those with access to magistracies: whatever the distinction between 'patricians' and 'plebeians' may originally have been, from 367/6 onwards powerful plebeian families had equal access to the supreme military offices with *imperium* (the authority to command). This new political élite, consisting of both patricians and

1

plebeians who justified their political control by their success as military commanders, was also persuaded to ameliorate the conditions of ordinary citizens (through the abolition of enslavement for debt during the Samnite Wars, and the establishing of settlements for landless Romans on conquered territory, e.g. in Cispadane Gaul), and to be liberal in granting citizenship to other individuals and communities, initially fellow-Latins but later some other Italians too, who had served Rome well. That willingness to share citizenship, exceptional in the ancient world, was itself another important factor in providing Rome with the manpower resources which enabled the Romans to win wars even when they had lost battles.

It was through warfare, therefore, that the Romans as a community won their primacy (the *maiestas populi Romani*) as well as the material benefits accruing from it. But individual Romans too won both wealth and public recognition (*gloria, honos*) through warfare. The principal component in the Roman understanding of what made a man excel, *virtus* ('manliness', conventionally translated as 'virtue'), was fighting ability. The fighting ability the Romans looked for was not simply the discipline and obedience required for success in the Greek hoplite phalanx: the conditions of fighting in the legion required the individual soldier to engage in hand-to-hand fighting. Hence the traditions of the republic emphasise stories (*exempla*) of individual combat: T. Manlius Torquatus, Catiline's ancestor Sergius, L. Siccius Dentatus (see Pliny, NH 7, 28/101-6). Many such anecdotes were exploited if not invented by later generations to augment the *virtus* they claimed to have inherited from their ancestors, but such stories continued to surface. The bravery of soldiers, and especially centurions, on both sides in Caesar's war against Pompey did not go unrecorded: e.g. Scaeva at Dyrrachium (Appian, BC 2, 9.60 = Caesar, BC 3, 53), or Crastinus at Pharsalus (Appian calls him Krassinios: BC 2, 11.82 = Caesar, BC 3, 91 and 99).

Roman culture celebrated, and depended upon, the fortitude of ordinary soldiers as well as their commanders. Military decorations, such as the crowns awarded for scaling an enemy wall or saving the life of a citizen, could be won equally by ordinary soldiers and by officers (like Julius Caesar: Suetonius, *Divus Julius* 2). Cicero puts into the mouth of Cato the Elder a list of famous Romans who showed courage in facing death or torture (*De Senectute* 20/75). But the climax of the passage is:

> Let us pass over these, and consider instead our invincible Roman legionaries. I have written of them in my *Origins*: these uneducated, rustic young soldiers march out again and again,

with indomitable enthusiasm, to destinations from which they expect never to return.

While the fighting ability of Rome's menfolk was the most important component of *virtus*, there were others. A famous speech given at the funeral of Lucius Caecilius Metellus in 221 listed ten. The catalogue is headed by 'being a warrior', followed by:

> ...being an outstanding public speaker; a most courageous general; one who won great military victories under his own auspices; holding the highest magistracies; having great wisdom; being considered the foremost senator; acquiring a lot of money honestly; leaving behind many children; and being held in great esteem by the community.
>
> (Pliny, NH 7, 43/139-40)

Lucius Metellus was one of the first great leaders of this famous plebeian family, holding the consulship in 251 and 247, and celebrating a triumph for his victories over the Carthaginians in Sicily. His *virtus* was not inherited, but personally achieved; and it will be noted that the list is in a sense chronological. Courage in the army and in the law courts in Metellus' youth led to successful military commands and magistracies; later in life, his activities centred on the Senate and on providing his household with wealth. Fame comes at the end.

Fig. 1 Coin minted by a Metellus c. 120 BC. The elephant became a symbol of the Metelli, since Lucius Metellus' triumph over the Carthaginians in 251 had been the first occasion on which elephants were displayed at Rome. While Lucius' fame had been personally earned, his descendants made political capital out of it.

Surviving funerary epitaphs support this picture of (at any rate public) virtue as founded upon military success and office-holding; many add public building. The epitaphs of the Scipios, now in the Lateran Museum in the Vatican, are mostly second-century BC revisions, detailing what made earlier members of the family so great. Of Lucius Scipio, who had been consul in 259, it is said:

> Honc oino ploirume cosentiont Romai
> Duonoro optimo fuise viro,
> Luciom Scipione. Filios Barbati
> Consul censor aidilis hic fuet apud vos.
> Hec cepit Corsica Aleriaque urbe.
> Dedet Tempestatebus aide meretod.

> [Most people at Rome agree that this one man was the best of good men, Lucius Scipio, son of Barbatus. He was consul, censor, and aedile among you. He captured Corsica and the city of Aleria. He gave a temple to the storm-gods in fulfilment of a vow.]

I have given the epitaph in Latin to make it clear just how different pre-classical Latin was from that which later became canonical, thanks in large measure to Cicero's own efforts.

While Roman *virtus* contained several components, military ability (at various levels) was so important that its too conspicuous achievement provoked suspicion and resentment in rival politicians. Exceptional *virtus* needed to be controlled, lest it destroy the 'level playing field' which was a precondition for the consent of those to whom the system did not bring pre-eminence. One way of preventing glory from becoming permanent was to put restrictions on the construction of public (or indeed private) monuments by individuals. Temples were permitted, and a very limited number of roads and aqueducts were constructed, mainly from the spoils won in victories. But until the first century, Rome had no permanent theatres for its public spectacles (except the Circus Maximus, which had been laid out by the kings; the Circus Flaminius is now thought to have been an open space, not a building). The short period of tenure of most offices was another way of limiting success, as was collegiality: at every level, those elected to magistracies found themselves with colleagues who might control and even prevent what they were doing.

Collegial pluralism also functioned to increase competition. Since there were fewer posts at the top of the hierarchy (the *cursus honorum*) than the bottom, some would necessarily fail to win election at each stage; so all tried to make the most of the opportunities that office-holding gave them, in winning friends or making money, or in using their *imperium* to win military victories whether they were necessary or not, since they might not get the chance to reach the next level in the *cursus*. The history of Roman wars in Spain in the second century BC illustrates the eagerness of the praetorian governors to win military glory in order to have a chance to be elected to the consulship on their return.

Magisterial collegiality had other considerable advantages for the community. It enabled the Romans to deal with wars on several fronts: in Cicero's early childhood, the Romans could deal in swift succession with Jugurtha in Numidia, the Cimbri in Gaul, a slave rebellion in Sicily, unrest in Greece and pirates in the eastern Mediterranean (see p. 18). In this respect, the monarchy established by Augustus proved less successful, when wars on several frontiers necessitated a split in the high command, as was to be shown by the instability of the third century AD, when each major army wanted to be led by its own emperor. But in the first century BC, political instability lay elsewhere. Its outward manifestation was the physical violence, the killing of political opponents, that marked political life in the city from the tribunates of the Gracchi on (134/3 and 124/2). Underlying the acceptability of violence was a breakdown in consensus about what was legitimate. In moral terms, the authority of 'good men' was no longer accepted because there was no longer agreement about what constituted *virtus*.

Authority had traditionally been located in the Senate, the repository of political experience. But the Senate necessarily always consisted of people who were suspicious of the successes of their rivals, and in whose interest it was to curb any individual politician who looked like being too successful. So far from being systematically imperialist, the Senate prevented its most successful military commanders from pursuing their military achievement too far. In the eastern Mediterranean, Lucius Scipio's victory over Antiochus the Great at the battle of Magnesia and the subsequent elimination of the Seleucid empire as a major power by the terms of the Treaty of Apamea resulted in a power vacuum. Wary of setting up new provinces which might become bases for excessive claims to military *virtus*, the Senate looked to local elites in the Greek cities, and to various local monarchs ('client kings' if they were recognised by Rome) to keep the peace. Where no local rulers were strong enough to do so – especially on the coasts of Cilicia – piracy flourished.

Apart from the pirates' direct victims, even those local leaders who wanted to remain on good terms with Rome suffered from the insecurity of living under the shadow of a republic in which no single individual was responsible for long-term policy. Rome did not accept the legitimacy of foreign dynasties, but only of particular individual kings, each of whom separately had to request the status of a 'king and ally and friend of the Roman people' (*Rex et socius ac amicus populi Romani*). Institutionally, client kings looked to the Senate for leadership, and for a long period in the second century BC the Senate successfully harnessed the expertise of its individual members to provide continuity in foreign policy. But in practice each king was the client of one or more particular Roman senators who represented his interests at Rome; and when in the first century BC the Senate's authority no longer sufficed to control some of these powerful Romans, the issue of who had Rome's friendship depended on the changing domestic position of Roman magnates. Strabo tells us how his ancestors had suffered when Pompey replaced Lucullus in Asia Minor, since 'Pompey treated as enemies all who had helped Lucullus, because of the hatred between them' (Strabo 12, 3.33). As Pompey put it before the battle of Pharsalus in 48 BC, 'All those kings who are friends of the Romans *or of myself*, are freely providing us with troops, weapons, provisions and other supplies' (Appian, BC 2, 8.51). When Pompey reflected on the best place to flee to after Pharsalus, he made no distinction between Numidia (whose king Juba I had been reinstated by Pompey in 81 BC), Egypt, and Parthia: all were equally sources of military and financial support for the individual who acted as their patron. Where there were no kings, local magnates secured their power through clientship with powerful Romans, and often used their local knowledge to provide assistance for military campaigns, especially with supplies. One such man was Cornelius Balbus from Gades (Cadiz) in Spain, who as *praefectus castrorum* supplied Caesar's Gallic armies and was to be rewarded with the first consulship held by a provincial; another was Theophanes of Mytilene, who provided the same service for Pompey. These clients did not serve the Roman republic but individual dynasts, in whose wake they rose or fell. The elite's competition for individual honour affected the entire empire.

Chapter 2
Competitiveness and the Creation of a Graeco-Roman Culture

Rome's competitive political culture motivated members of the élite to launch into the wars of conquest which established the Roman empire, but it also took more pacific forms. Wealthy men competed in seeking the approval of the people by providing it with public spectacles like the gladiatorial games which were beginning to become so popular in the late second century, or with the comedies of Plautus and Terence which were performed at religious festivals (ludi). The frequency with which Cicero refers to gladiators in his speeches, and uses quotations from Terence's comedies or Accius' tragedies, illustrates how acquaintance with public spectacles could be taken for granted in a Roman audience of whatever status. The speeches which Cicero and his rivals performed at public open-air trials in the Roman forum were spectacles with much the same function, at least from the orator's point of view. Hence there were attempts to put restrictions on Latin oratory as late as 95 BC, just as there were limitations on other kinds of shows. The greatest spectacle of all was the triumph; that especially was hedged around with controls, and brought glory for only one day. Spectacular displays of the wealth that came from success, even military success, were liable to bring disapproval. Lucullus (who died in 56) spent his wealth on banquets, and became notorious for luxus, displaying his wealth immorally.

Another way of competing for status was through scholarship. Patrician families had maintained their place at the political centre through their knowledge of the arcane forms and procedures required by Roman law. Such knowledge was one of the ways in the late republic in which a patrician with no recent political background like Servius Sulpicius Rufus (cos. 51: see Cicero's Pro Murena) could find his way back to the centre of things. Antiquarianism, the claim to study the remote origins of Roman, and increasingly Italian, institutions, was also a source of prestige. It could be associated with claims about the antiquity of one's own family, and at a more sophisticated level with the search for an authentic and pure Latinity, which some (including Julius Caesar

7

and Varro) claimed was superior to the uncritical use of Greek verbal techniques, commonplaces and loanwords by rivals like Cicero, who were accused of being 'Asianists'. What looks to us like a leisure activity was an aspect of élite competition. The same applied to writing works of literature: this was obvious in the production of epics or prose narratives on contemporary history (e.g. Cicero's glorification of his consulship, or the poet Archias' epic honouring Lucullus), but in a different way it might even be true of writing love-poetry. Q. Lutatius Catulus (cos.102) claimed an equal role with Marius in defeating the Cimbri at Vercellae; when he demonstrated his knowledge of Greek literature by writing Latin love poetry, he was claiming to be Marius' superior. Not surprisingly, Marius was said to have been scathing about the predilection for Greek culture of politicians from established families (cf. Sallust, *Jugurtha* 85.32).

Knowledge of Greek literature gave certain individuals a claim to high status. By its nature, foreign knowledge is only accessible to a limited number of people with unusual educational opportunities (e.g. family links abroad, or the ownership of educated slaves). Those who have made use of these opportunities can then claim to be superior to others of the same background and class. Since at least the third century BC philhellenism had been exploited by Roman senators in their competition for status with their rivals. Notable instances in Cicero's time were Lucullus and Hortensius. Lucullus' case shows that philhellenism and military virtue were alternatives that did not exclude each other, and Hortensius' case shows that someone deeply influenced by one branch of Greek culture (rhetoric) might deny the relevance of another branch (philosophy) in which he was not as competent as his rival, Cicero.

One of the disadvantages of political competition was that individuals selected fashions for their short-term advantage to themselves, and tended to have little or no interest in the good of non-Romans, rivals, or even (in spite of their patriotic rhetoric) the community. Instead of investing in public buildings, the emphasis was on short-term spectacles. At the political level, no individual was responsible for long-term policy-making; the Senate certainly contained men of experience, whose advice magistrates were obliged to take into consideration, but only the magistrates were answerable for their actions, and they only had the responsibility to act during their term of office (normally one year). The lack of any central financial control became particularly obvious after the Social War (91/89), when the costs of providing Rome's armies more than doubled (because the Italian allies were no longer responsible for contributing separate contingents). Particular individuals could exploit their financial expertise to reach a position of eminence (Lucullus, Crassus). One of the foundations of the absolute political control exercised by Augustus and his successors was that their private wealth (the *domus Caesaris*) and the funds they controlled as magistrates (the *fiscus*) were sufficient to enable them to plan policy without reference to the state *aerarium* (treasury) and the Senate which controlled it.

But even Augustus, and certainly Cicero's contemporaries Crassus, Lucullus, Pompey and Caesar, had long-term 'policies' in the modern sense only in a very limited respect. There were no academic think-tanks or policy study groups; there were no interest-groups with long-term aims – even the *publicani*, companies who bid for state contracts, only had agreements which lasted for five years. Policies, or proposals for new legislation, therefore tended to be short-term bids for popularity and esteem, like providing the electorate with games, or delivering a stunning speech. Not surprisingly, some of the political questions which Roman politicians used to win support were as artificial as political issues in the modern world: e.g. the belief that Rome's manpower was declining, or that there was a conflict between senators and those labelled 'equestrians' (both issues were seized on by the Gracchi, and bedevilled the politics of the next half-century). On the other hand the language in which these issues were publicly presented emphasised the primacy of the public good over that of individuals and interest-groups, and all but a few politicians – then as now – will have perceived their actions as aiming at the good of the community. But it is not unduly cynical to consider that if alongside immediate popularity Roman politicians also had long-term aims, these included not just the success (especially military) of Rome, but also concentrating wealth, glory, and patronage in the hands of their own direct descendants.

For Romans, there was no clear dividing line between patronage and friendship (*amicitia*). In this period formal, legally-recognised patronage – *patrocinium* – generally applied only to the relationship between a freed slave and his former owner, and between a non-Roman community and the Roman who represented its interests at Rome. In a pre-industrial world, where the state gave no social support and there was not even any real mechanism for providing financial credit, people of every status needed friends to help with advice, loans, recommendations to others ('brokerage'), health care, education for their children, support in old age, and occasionally protection against those more powerful than themselves. One of a friend's duties was to speak on your behalf when you had to go to law: on this occasion the orator was actually called by the traditional word *patronus*.

Friendship had political implications. A citizen, even if he had nothing else to give his 'friend', could vote for him (or his political allies) at elections, and could increase his friend's prestige by applauding his speeches or accompanying him, especially when he left and entered the city. But these networks were not like political parties: everyone tried to have as many friends as possible, and when there were conflicts between them, obligations to both sides gave the option to support neither. Even family relationships do not necessarily create political groupings: sons may disagree with their fathers (e.g. the Curios), and brothers have notoriously been hostile to each other since Cain and Abel. But while brothers may have conflicting interests (particularly, in a world with no primogeniture, on questions of inheritance), and may adopt different political strategies (e.g. Appius Claudius the consul of 54, and his brother Clodius), they may still be prepared to protect each other in a crisis.

Despite the emphasis on women's studies in recent years, much academic work remains to be done on family relationships through women as wives and mothers. Their role was not just to be a symbol of disorder, as in Catiline's conspiracy, when he was provided with money by 'women who hoped that their husbands would be killed' (Appian, BC 2, 1.2; cf. Sallust, *Catiline* 24). The civil wars of the first century BC created widows, who under Roman law controlled households in their own right, and exiled men, whose mothers or wives acted on their behalf (as Terentia did for Cicero – even during his governorship of Cilicia; cf. also Appian, BC 1, 7.63). Marriage could also give an able politician access to inherited property, and to the inherited political capital represented by 'friendship'.

An inherited family tradition, real or fabricated, was as much political capital as wealth. Cato the Younger could lay claim to moral superiority because his great-grandfather had been a stern censor (Plutarch says that the Elder Cato claimed that where others competed in wealth or avarice, he competed in *virtus*: *Cato Maior* 19.5), and M. Junius Brutus by virtue of descent from the man who had expelled the last king from Rome. Cicero had no such ancestors; his claim to the moral high ground was based on his superior knowledge of Greek philosophy, which gave him an insight into a 'Natural Justice' more valid than the right which 'popular' politicians (*populares*) claimed resided in legislation which they forced through the assemblies, or even the ancestral custom to which the political establishment (the 'optimates' or 'best people') appealed.

The different claims to legitimacy which politicians exploited in their struggle for short-term advantage resulted in a lack of consensus

Fig. 2 Statue of a Roman holding the busts (*imagines*) of two of his ancestors as a claim to his own nobility.

about the limits of acceptable behaviour – in other words a crisis in political morality. The temptation to use force rather than persuasion, bribery or social authority to achieve a favourable vote led to gang warfare, the assassination of political rivals, and ultimately, for those who saw no other way of achieving glory, violent uprisings against the established regime. In this respect, there was no difference between Sulla, Catiline, and Caesar.

Warfare had been crucial to the Romans' self-identity since the fourth century BC. Wars of conquest abroad had been one way in which Roman leaders competed with one another. It had been a means of keeping the Roman community united through the shared process of conquering the rest of the Mediterranean world. Since Roman armies before the Social War were generally made up of 60% Italian allies and only 40% Roman citizens, that process also united Romans and Italians (who, from the standpoint of provincials, increasingly came to be seen as one people). By the middle of the second century BC, Italian soldiers, and the local leaders who led them on campaign, felt increasing resentment at the way they were being excluded from the benefits of the empire they were helping Rome to win. After 170, the Romans ceased founding colonies of Latin status in which the allies were allowed to participate; and after the overthrow of King Perseus in 167 the tribute payments which the Romans imposed on Macedonia enabled them to remit direct taxes on Roman land, while the allies had to continue to pay for their own army contingents. The question of how to integrate the Italians became acute, and was there to be exploited by Roman politicians in the course of their competition with one another. Only when many of the allied communities started the military rebellion known as the Social War in 90 BC did the Romans recognise that the problem had to be resolved by granting Roman citizenship to every community in Italy.

The effects of the Social War, by transferring the loyalties of Italian soldiers from their local leaders to the Roman generals to whom they swore obedience and whom they would need to provide them with land when their campaigning was over, resulted in massive social deracination as former soldiers were settled far from their places of origin. 'Our provinces are full of people very few of whom ever return to their town of origin', says Cicero (*Tusculans* 5, 36/105). The social dislocation was made worse by Sulla's subsequent proscriptions, which resulted in significant changes in the ownership of landed estates (as illustrated in some of Cicero's speeches). Large country estates came to be auctioned at Rome, not in the local forum (cf. Cicero's *Pro Caecina*). Individuals found themselves owning property in several Italian cities, and marriages between families whose homes were hundreds of miles apart became common. The land-owning élite of Italy soon came to see itself as one single Latin-speaking community, rather than two hundred or so individual cities and tribes with different languages and identities. That new and artificial community needed new cultural symbols, and they were taken from the entire range which competing Roman leaders had to offer: the promise of world empire, gladiatorial games, a common system of law, a wider Latin vocabulary to express the technical terms of Greek scholarship, a corpus of poetry to rival Greece (i.e. Catullus, Lucretius, Vergil, Propertius, Horace and the other 'classics'), and of course oratory. No one planned the long-term effect of these competing strategies for glory; as with most social and cultural revolutions – including that leading to the creation of a new pan-European culture in our own generation – few, even of the intellectuals, saw why a new culture was needed. But there were some who did see that it was needed, and Cicero was perhaps better than any at realising his personal ambitions by providing what the unification of Italy called for.

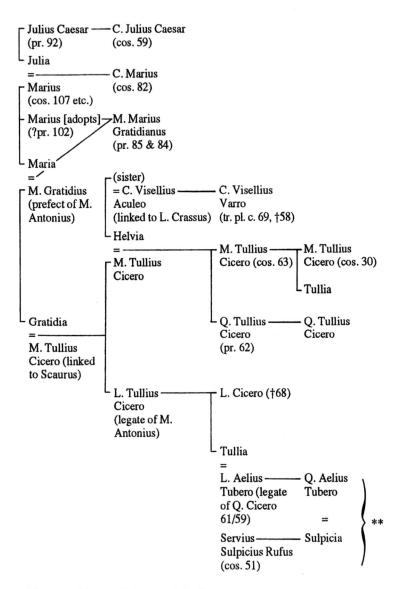

The symbol '=' stands for 'married to'.
pr. stands for praetor.
** For Tubero's children and grandchildren, see R. Syme, *The Augustan Aristocracy* (Oxford, 1986), stemmata xxiii and xxiv.

Fig. 3 Stemma I: Cicero's family links.

Chapter 3
New Men and Old Families

When Cicero was born at Arpinum on 3rd January 106, one of the dominant political figures at Rome was Marcus Aemilius Scaurus; since his consulship in 115, he was *princeps senatus*, the recognised senior senator. Although Scaurus was a patrician, his family had played no known political role for some generations; he won public office relatively late in life (he appears to have been born c. 163/2), as a result of an alliance with the most powerful plebeian family of the late second century, the Metelli. His fellow-consul in 115 was a Metellus, and his wife was the daughter of Metellus Delmaticus (consul 119; so named for a triumph over the Dalmatians in 117). Scaurus had three children by her, and after his death she was to marry Sulla, to whom she bore his twins Fausta and Faustus.

While Scaurus was at the very centre of the political establishment, he also looked for support from men of ability from families outside that establishment. One of the municipalities with which he had particular links of patronage was Arpinum: one of the praetors in 115 was the Arpinate Gaius Marius, and although he was later represented as an opponent of the Metelli (who did not support his ambition to stand for the consulship), he started his political career as their protégé. Although Cicero consistently distanced himself from Marius in his political writings, his pride in the achievements of his fellow-townsman is shown by the fact that he wrote a poem in Marius' praise, to which he refers in his dialogue *De Legibus*. In the same dialogue, Cicero also refers proudly to Scaurus' approval in the Senate of the political position taken by Cicero's grandfather in municipal politics at Arpinum (in opposition to the introduction of secret ballots at elections):

> With your courage and ability, Marcus Cicero, I wish that you had preferred to be active at the political centre rather than at the municipal level.
>
> (*De Legibus* 3.16/36)

Scaurus failed to persuade Cicero's grandfather that his future lay in Rome, but he had other protégés from Arpinum – he dedicated the three volumes of his political memoirs to someone called Fufidius; and a bronze tablet recently discovered at Alcantara mentions a Lucius Caesius who governed Nearer Spain as praetor in 104. Both the Fufidii and the Caesii are known from Cicero's letters to have been prominent Arpinum families; Lucius Caesius is likely to have been another of Scaurus' supporters. It is not surprising that Cicero should have referred to Scaurus in the most positive terms in both speeches and rhetorical works (esp. *Brutus* 110-16).

Arpinum had not originally been a Latin-speaking city at all. As late as 305, it was fighting Rome on the Samnite side, and was captured in a siege; two years later the Romans gave it *civitas sine suffragio*, the status of permanent subjection entailing the duties but not the political rights of citizens (Livy 9, 44.16). In 188 it was made a Roman municipality with full citizenship. This was an unusual privilege; one possible explanation for it is that soldiers from Arpinum, like those from the neighbouring city of Fregellae, had played a conspicuous role in the course of the war against the Seleucid king Antiochus III in 192/190. For whatever reason, by the time that Cicero was born Arpinum's élite families used Latin as their everyday language and were well on the way to complete integration into the Roman political system.

The personal nature of Roman politics meant that once one man from a particular place had won influence at the centre, he often brought his friends (and competitors) with him: under the principate, this was to apply in turn to the appearance at Rome of groups of senators, soldiers and writers from Spain, southern Gaul, and Africa. While Cicero's paternal grandfather was associated with Scaurus, his political opponent – and his wife's brother – Marcus Gratidius was the protégé of another important political leader, Marcus Antonius. When Antonius was sent to Cilicia as praetor in 102, Gratidius was a member of his staff; so was a nephew, Lucius, Cicero's uncle. Other links with the Roman élite were strengthened through marriages. Cicero's cousin Tullia (Lucius' daughter) married a Lucius Aelius Tubero (one of the legates of Cicero's brother Quintus in Asia in 58), of a family of legal experts. Their son Quintus Aelius Tubero married the daughter of the greatest jurist of Cicero's time, Servius Sulpicius Rufus. (A granddaughter of Quintus, Aelia Paetina, was to marry the later emperor Claudius.) A sister of Cicero's mother Helvia married C. Visellius Aculeo, linked to another leading Roman politician, L. Licinius Crassus. Gratidius' wife was a sister of Marius. Marius had been consul in 107, the year before Cicero's

Fig. 4 A city gate at Arpinum. The massive defences built in the late fourth century BC bear witness to Arpinum's pre-Roman, Volscian past.

birth, and had taken over command of the war against the Numidian client-king Jugurtha from his erstwhile patron, Metellus Numidicus. Conflict between Scaurus and Metellus on the one hand, and Marius and his supporters on the other, coloured the politics of Cicero's childhood. He remembered how his father spoke about the attempt to try Metellus for extortion, 'when I was a boy' (*Pro Balbo* 5.11). Scaurus only just avoided conviction in an extortion trial, and retaliated by accusing Marius' fellow-consul in 104, C. Flavius Fimbria.

Fig. 5 Coin showing Marius' triumph over the Cimbri and Teutones (101 BC). Marius' son, who had considerable responsibility for the massacres of the 80s, is shown riding on the lead horse.

Since the murder of Tiberius Gracchus in 133, political conflicts had led to violence, especially when popular support for a particular cause was mobilised by a plebeian tribune. In 100, a tribune, L. Appuleius Saturninus, was killed. In the course of a personal feud against Scaurus and the Metelli (the censors Metellus Numidicus and Metellus Caprarius had tried to expel Saturninus from the Senate in 102), Saturninus had exploited the very serious military difficulties that faced Rome during these years. As well as fighting wars against Jugurtha, a separatist kingdom ruled by the ex-slave Salvius in Sicily, and the Cilician pirates, the Romans were faced with an invasion of southern Gaul by a Germanic tribe called the Cimbri. In 105, they defeated a Roman army at Arausio. This required the rapid deployment of newly raised and newly trained soldiers by Marius and his fellow-consul, Rutilius Rufus. Following Marius' victories over the Teutones at Aquae Sextiae in 102 and the Cimbri at Vercellae in northern Italy in the following year, Saturninus proposed to make land available in a number of new colonies for these soldiers, and he included provisions for people of Latin and Italian status as well as full Roman citizens. His assassination only temporarily removed from the political agenda the question of the relationship between the Roman state and the allied soldiers upon whom the Romans now clearly depended for the defence of Italy.

When Cicero's parents decided to groom their two sons for the metropolitan career that his grandfather had rejected, their wide range of family links allowed them to avoid dangerous associations. Cicero, his brother Quintus (four years younger), and paternal cousin Lucius, were not sent for their training in public life either to Scaurus or his Metellan friends, or to Marius. The links they exploited were associations through Cicero's grandmother with Antonius and mother with Crassus. (*De Oratore* 2.1 has much information about the teenager's impressions of this period.)

L. Licinius Crassus had been consul in 95, and then went on to govern Transalpine Gaul. Cicero presumably joined his entourage in 93, when he was censor with Cn. Domitius Ahenobarbus. One of their acts was to shut down a school of Latin oratory recently opened by a Marian supporter, L. Plotius Gallus. In the political climate of the time, the censors were afraid that expertise in Latin rhetoric might be used further to inflame the political situation. But that did not mean that Crassus was hostile to rhetorical culture. He had studied Greek rhetorical theory, and practised Greek-type exercises (*De Oratore* 1.137ff., 154ff.). And he put his theoretical knowledge into practice. One of his legal speeches on a question of inheritance became particularly famous as the so-called *Causa Curiana*, and is worth considering at some length. It was delivered in c. 93, and strongly influenced Cicero's attitude to the relationship between oratory and the law; he was probably present at the hearing before the Centumviral Court. Crassus was opposed by the leading legal expert of the time, Scaevola the Pontifex (consul with Crassus in 95). Scaevola took a literal interpretation of a clause in a will which instituted a certain Manius Curius as the testator's substitute heir should his (as yet unborn) children die. The testator in fact died without ever having had any children, and Scaevola argued that the will was therefore strictly speaking invalid: there could be no heir to a child who had never been born (*pupillo non nato heredem esse non posse*). By mobilising extra-legal principles of equity culled from Greek moral philosophy, as well as a great deal of humour, Crassus was able to persuade the jury to ignore the letter of the law in favour of what were the testator's obvious intentions. It is a sign of the late republic's confusion about moral and legal values that Crassus could persuade a jury to ignore the law. It is even more remarkable that later Roman law recognised Crassus' arguments as valid.

Crassus died in 91, when Cicero was fifteen; he had supported an attempt by the tribune M. Livius Drusus to grant citizenship more widely to Latin and Italian allies, and had spoken so vehemently against the consul L. Marcius Philippus that he succumbed to pneumonia in consequence of physical exhaustion. Cicero's other mentor in political life, Marcus Antonius, was also to die while Cicero was still in his teens (at the hands of the Marians in 87, though he had earlier been close to Marius and his supporters). As praetor in 102, Antonius had been sent east, as we have seen, against the Cilician pirates (with Cicero's great-uncle M. Gratidius and uncle Lucius on his staff). Copies of his decree against piracy have been found at Cnidos and Delphi. On the way, he provided Athens with a new constitution, anchoring political control in the hands of the local élite through the council of ex-magistrates, the Areopagus. Antonius celebrated a triumph in 100, and was censor in 97.

Unlike Crassus, Antonius represented his ability as primarily that of a successful fighting man, and he tried to disguise his knowledge of Greek literature; although he actually wrote a book on oratory, he claimed that it was based on experience, not on the theory of the schools (*De Oratore* 1.94; 208; cf. the attitude ascribed to Marius by Sallust, *Jugurtha* 63.3 and 85.31f.). Cicero will have heard some of his rhetorical outbursts, e.g. when he evoked sympathy for an ex-soldier of Marius' during the extortion trial of Manius Aquilius (consul 101) by appealing 'to every god, man, citizen and ally' (*De Oratore* 2.194-6). What Antonius had in common with Crassus was a marked disrespect for legal niceties. Not only was he ignorant of law; he claimed that this ignorance was no disadvantage (*De Oratore* 1.172 and 248). In his speeches, he lied and contradicted himself to such an extent that he refused to publish anything, in case he was unmasked (*Pro Cluentio* 140; cf. Valerius Maximus 7, 3.5). In a speech defending Saturninus' supporter Norbanus in 94 he successfully argued that violence could be justified because it had in the past led to constitutional improvements (*De Oratore* 2.199) – a particularly frightening symptom of the dissolution of constitutional norms in the late republic.

Antonius' cavalier attitude to legality was in marked contrast to that of another person with whom the young Cicero associated, Mucius Scaevola the Augur (consul 117; died 87). Crassus, Antonius and Scaevola are the three main characters in Cicero's dialogue *De Oratore*, the dramatic date of which is 91. Scaevola the Augur was a distant relative of Scaevola the Pontifex (see p. 19 above), and, like other members of the family, emphasised the importance of knowledge of the law; he criticised contemporaries like Galba, Lepidus and Carbo for their legal ignorance, and was as prepared to justify Saturninus' murder as he was to impugn Sulla's banishment of Marius on strictly legal grounds. Scaevola was married to Laelia, the daughter of the younger Scipio's friend Laelius; it will have been through Scaevola that Cicero built up a picture of Scipio and his friends as philhellene intellectuals. The idea that Scipio Aemilianus' friends constituted a formal 'Scipionic Circle' is largely a construct of nineteenth-century scholarship; but a generation later Scaevola's house was indeed frequented by Greek philosophers such as Philo the Sceptic.

However 'Roman' Crassus, Antonius and Scaevola might have wanted to appear in public, Cicero learnt from them that there was a wealth of technical knowledge and rhetorical tricks to be acquired from Greek literature. Cicero applied himself to the study of Greek, and declaimed (practised model speeches) in Greek rather than Latin, 'with Marcus Piso and Quintus Pompeius' (*Brutus* 309f.). To perfect his knowledge of Greek, he translated two of the most widely-read works of Greek poetry and prose, Aratus' *Phaenomena* and Xenophon's *Oeconomicus*. Years later they were to resurface as material for his philosophical works. In his biography of Cicero, Plutarch, who came from Boeotia, also picks out a poem Cicero composed about a Boeotian hero, Pontios Glaukos. Plutarch believed that the young Cicero dedicated himself to Greek learning so fully that his contemporaries called him a Greek. In fact, Cicero constantly makes it clear in his writings how much superior he thought the Roman character was to the Greek. Plutarch was wrong in thinking that young Cicero wanted to become a philosopher. He had been sent to Crassus and Antonius in order to learn how to become a Roman politician. Greek knowledge was of interest in the first instance because it widened the armoury of weapons open to Roman politicians.

In 91 that armoury once again included violence. The tribune M. Livius Drusus made a number of proposals which were opposed by the consul L. Marcius Philippus and others; one of these proposals was to solve the Italian problem by granting Roman citizenship to all Italian allies. Some of the allies, under the leadership of the Marsian Q. Poppaedius Silo, were prepared to support Drusus' proposal by force. When he was killed in the ensuing violence, their disappointment turned to open military rebellion, in what the Romans officially termed the 'Marsian' war, but is normally called the Social War, the war between Rome and many of her Italian allies.

Fig. 6 Coin struck by the Italian allies during the Social War. The bull, representing Italy (Vitellus = bull) gores the Roman wolf.

It was clear what those allied communities which took up arms, mainly in the centre and south of Italy, wanted: an end to the system whereby the major costs of the Roman war machine were borne by Italians, but neither the soldiers nor their leaders had equal access to the profits of empire, and the communities as a whole still had to pay for their contingents, even though Roman citizens had been exempted from supporting the army through taxation ever since the time when Macedonia had been conquered in 167 BC. The inferior status of the allies in Roman eyes led to instances of disgraceful treatment by Roman magistrates: on one notorious occasion, the chief magistrate of Teanum Sidicinum was flogged because he was slow in getting the city's baths ready for the wife of a visiting consul (Aulus Gellius 10, 3.2). But few if any of the Italian communities, even the Samnites, wanted total independence: the coins depicting the Italian bull aggressively goring the Roman wolf were intended to encourage soldiers fighting what was in effect a civil war. The joint command and joint senate set up by the allies at Corfinium were the organs of a temporary alliance, not of a long-term 'federal' government. What they wanted was to replace the Roman monopoly of power with an Italy which was federal only in the sense that none of its leaders would be excluded from that power. As it was, the chieftains of some Italian communities saw more disadvantages than advantages in accepting Roman laws and customs. In Etruria, the aristocratic clans which had presided over the development of urban culture for the past six or seven centuries had jealously guarded their political privileges against encroachments by a rural population whose legal status was quasi-servile: they did not relish the extension of civic rights which would accompany a grant of Roman citizenship. The princes of Etruria generally kept their cities out of the Social War.

Chapter 4
The Army in Politics

The transformation of the Roman army from a citizen levy of peasants conscripted for a particular campaign into an army of semi-professionals appears to have been a much more gradual process than scholars once believed. One important stage in this development were the so-called 'Marian reforms' (actually the rapid training programme introduced by the consul Rufus in 105). By Marius' time, some of the men who were enlisted were not property-owners (*assidui*) with smallholdings to which they would be able to return after their period of military service was over. Such men had chosen to join a particular general in the hope that he would employ them for several campaigning seasons, and began to look to him to provide them with land at the end of their period of service.

The brutality of the Social War may be explained as much by the fact that it was fought by experienced professionals as that it was fought between former comrades-in-arms. Both the shift away from a citizen to a career army, and the war's brutality, are demonstrated by Appian's catalogue of encounters during the war which resulted in very high casualties; the list ends with a reference to the Senate's decision to end the custom of having the bodies of the fallen returned to Rome for burial, 'so that the rest would not be discouraged by the spectacle' (τοῦ μὴ τοὺς λοιποὺς ἐκ τῆς οψεως ἀποτρέπεσθαι, Appian, BC 1, 5.43). Even after death, soldiers were now looked after by their commanders, not by the Roman state; and the experience of the Social War directly prepared Roman armies for the civil wars that followed.

For a young Roman who aimed at a career in public life, military service was not optional, though by Cicero's time it no longer needed to last for a period of years. Cicero's participation as a military tribune on the staff of the consul Pompeius Strabo has left an epigraphical trace. He is listed with many others, including Lucius Sergius Catilina (whose first wife was a sister of Marius Gratidianus), as being present in Pompeius' advisory council (*consilium*) when a contingent of Spanish cavalry was granted the privilege of Roman citizenship as a reward for its help in the fighting. Later he served with Sulla at the siege of Nola in Campania (*De Divinatione*). By this stage the Roman élite had come to realise that their hegemony could only be preserved if the allies were granted the citizenship they wanted; this was done through a *Lex Julia* in 90 and a *Lex Plautia Papiria* in 89 which granted citizenship to those who had remained loyal, but provided for them to be registered in only ten of the thirty-five tribal units. This would have had the effect of minimising the electoral advantage to those Roman politicians – like Pompeius Strabo – who would be the patrons of the new voters; but it also unnecessarily kept the issue on the political agenda. Cicero records how in 88 he heard the tribune P. Sulpicius speak in favour of allowing the Italians to be registered in all the tribes equally, and attacking the consul Sulla. Sulpicius' campaign against Sulla led directly to the first occasion on which a Roman army rejected senatorial authority.

Mithridates VI, the king of Pontus in northern Anatolia, had a long-standing claim to control the neighbouring kingdom of Cappadocia, which he had occupied in 104, exploiting Rome's defeat at Arausio. The Senate had forced him to give up the territory in 95, but during the Social War he re-occupied it together with the rival kingdom of Bithynia (long a Roman client kingdom), and then he went on to invade the Roman province of Asia and European Greece itself. With the Social War over, the Senate authorised the consul Sulla to lead his army of six legions east to reclaim Bithynia. However, in order to obtain Marius' support for his legislation, Sulpicius proposed transferring the command against Mithridates to Marius. In the ensuing rioting, Sulla could only save his life by taking refuge in Marius' own house, and acquiescing in the transfer of command. While almost all Sulla's officers accepted the legislation, the legionaries did not. The new conditions of fighting had made them Sulla's soldiers, and they were afraid that the campaign against Mithridates would be assigned to others. So they followed Sulla against Rome, where he had Marius and Sulpicius declared public enemies, and himself re-appointed to the eastern command. He then took his army to Greece.

After Sulla's departure, political life at Rome continued much as before. Apart from unsuccessfully attempting to transfer command of Pompeius Strabo's army to a supporter of his own, Sulla had not appointed his own supporters to public office but merely made the consuls-elect swear that they would not rescind his enactments. But in 87 one of them, Cornelius Cinna, re-introduced Sulpicius' proposal on the citizenship, and when it was opposed occupied Rome with soldiers from the former allied communities. He also brought back Marius, who was declared consul for the seventh and last time for 86, and died a few days after taking office. Marius' return was accompanied by a settling of scores, particularly by his son: many of the old political leaders who

had treated him so badly in the past, if they had not already died like
Aemilius Scaurus, were killed, including Antonius, P. Crassus (father of
the 'triumvir'), L. Domitius Ahenobarbus and, in 82, Scaevola the
Pontifex. Nevertheless the regime of Cinna and his associate Cn. Papi-
rius Carbo was generally obeyed in Italy and the West until 83.

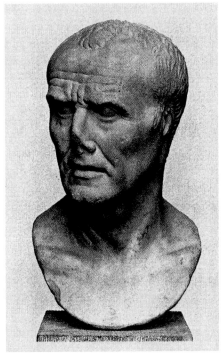

Fig. 7 Bust of Marius.

After the Social War, Cicero joined the entourage of Scaevola the
Augur (*Brutus* 306), together with his friends Atticus and Servius
Sulpicius Rufus , primarily in order to gain experience of legal rules and
procedures. The **De Inventione**, his first essay on rhetoric, is generally
thought to date to the early 80s (because Antonius is not mentioned, and
was therefore either still alive, or too unpopular with those in power).
Cicero later describes it as based on the notebooks of his youth, and tries
to excuse its lack of sophistication: he explicitly wanted it to be superseded by the later *De Oratore*. *De Inventione* is a handbook on material
for the public speaker, listing arguments that can be used in each 'type'
or category of issue. It was an important text in the Middle Ages, when

it was known as the *Rhetorica Prima*; the *Rhetorica Secunda* was what is now known as the anonymous *Rhetorica ad Herennium*, another treatise probably dating to the 80s and based on lecture-notes. The contrast is interesting. Cicero's version reveals a greater interest in philosophy: thus the introduction emphasises the importance of uniting philosophical knowledge with rhetorical skill (a point Cicero was to repeat in later rhetorical treatises), pointing to Cato, the Gracchi, Scipio and Laelius as Roman precedents for such a combination. The reference to the Gracchi fits well with the period when politics was dominated by Cinna, Carbo, and the younger Marius; one is also tempted to assume that Cicero's poem on Marius was written in this period, though it was not held against him after Sulla's return.

Mithridates VI's occupation of Greece and abolition of some of the aristocratic regimes which had supported the Romans – including that imposed on Athens by Antonius in 102 – resulted in the arrival at Rome of a number of wealthy refugees from Athens who preferred to put their trust in Roman might rather than in liberation (and democratisation) by Mithridates. One of them was the Academic (Sceptic) philosopher Philo, who joined Scaevola's household in 88; perhaps his lectures provided some of the material behind the *De Inventione*. Other possible influences were Aelius Stilo and the Stoic philosopher Diodotus, who came to live with Cicero (*Brutus* 309). Diodotus emphasised that a public speaker needed not only technical ability, but also a command of information. While, as we have seen, Greek culture was a means to political success, the claim to be dedicating oneself to the theoretical life of philosophy had its advantages in a period of political uncertainty.

Uncertainty turned to civil war again with Sulla's return after he had successfully expelled Mithridates from Greece and from the Asian territories he had occupied. When he arrived in Italy, Sulla was soon joined by those barred from politics by the Marian regime. With their help he overthrew the legitimate government even though it was given substantial support by former allies in Etruria and other parts of Italy. A battle outside the Colline Gate at Rome in September 82 effectively ended the war, though Volaterrae in Etruria held out for two more years.

Instead of reconciliation, the *Sullani* (Sulla's supporters) wanted revenge for themselves or their murdered relatives. Sulla drew up a list of those who had forfeited their claim to citizen rights which is said originally to have contained the names of 40 senators and 1,600 equestrians; once others had been added, with or without the approval or knowledge of Sulla himself, the final figure was reported as 90 senators (15 of them consulars) and 2,600 equestrians (Appian, *BC* 1, 11.95 and 12.103).

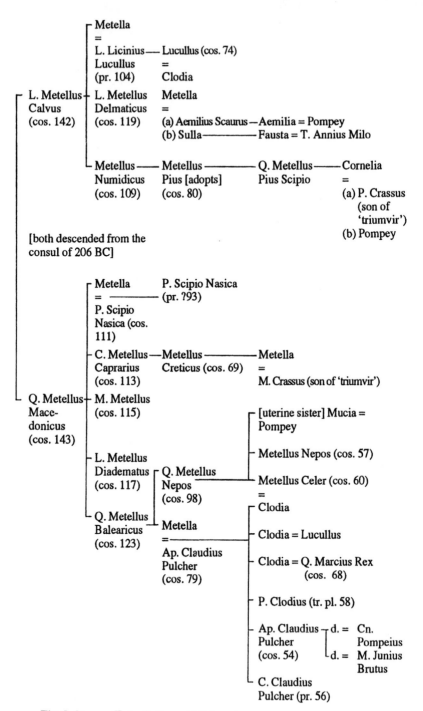

Fig. 8 Stemma II: the Sullan establishment.

Chapter 5
The Sullan Regime

Modern historians have tended to see Sulla's rule as representing a coherent political line, the restoration of aristocratic or senatorial rule (the two are not necessarily identical). But Sulla and his supporters were like other Roman political coalitions. What united them was not a common programme, let alone a 'party' organisation, but perceived common interests; and as with other Roman coalitions, these were short-term interests. On his return to Italy, Sulla gathered together those who had been excluded during the 80s from what were, or what they thought were, their legitimate rights and honours. There were great differences among them; they were united by the hope that Sulla's army would be strong enough to overcome the Marian regime, and by joining him they of course increased his chances of success.

Sulla's four most important military supporters were L. Licinius Lucullus, who was his quaestor in the East and had been largely responsible for finding the resources for defeating Mithridates; Pompey (Gn. Pompeius, later surnamed 'Magnus', the Great), son of Pompeius Strabo; Metellus Pius, son of Marius' patron and opponent Metellus Numidicus; and M. Licinius Crassus, son of the consul of 97 BC. These men were long-term rivals as well as short-term allies; their lack of personal loyalty to Sulla is best illustrated by Pompey's insistence that he be given further military commands (in Africa and Spain) in direct contravention of Sulla's regulations to control independent military power-bases. Other *Sullani* were equally unruly: Sulla felt obliged to have one of them, Lucretius, killed in the Roman forum.

Not all of Sulla's associates based their claim to authority on traditional Roman military virtues. In particular, Quintus Hortensius Hortalus (born 114), had been educated in Greek culture and wrote literature, including an epic history of the Social War and some love poetry (he is referred to in Catullus 65 and 95). He was also the orator who, before Cicero, made the greatest use of Greek rhetorical theory. Later Cicero was to describe Hortensius' style as 'Asianist', i.e. containing too many and inappropriate Greek techniques. Many years later, at the trial of Publius Sulla, the prosecutor Lucius Torquatus was to accuse Hortensius of being not just an actor, but a pantomime and even a 'Dionysia' (a notorious dancing girl of the time). Hortensius is said to have had the courage to reply: 'I would certainly rather be like Dionysia, Torquatus, than be without the Muses, without Aphrodite, and uncongenial (ἄμουσος ἀναφρόδιτος ἀπροσδιόνυσος), like you' – a remarkable instance of the acceptance of Greek values by a member of the late republican élite, even to the extent of using the Greek language at a Roman political trial, something hard to imagine either earlier or later (Aulus Gellius 1, 5.3).

Although Sulla and his supporters in general rejected any compromise or reconciliation with those who had ruled before them, there was one pragmatic exception: it was in the interests of Rome's security to integrate Italian soldiers fully, rather than leave them as the clients of local leaders like those who had supported Cinna at the battle of the Colline Gate. So Sulla maintained the right of Italians to be registered in all thirty-five tribes, thus removing the issue of citizenship from the agenda once and for all (though later politicians, especially Caesar, were to raise it again for the communities of Cisalpine Gaul). One effect of this political integration of Italians was that henceforth they would look for political leadership beyond their local leaders to those Roman politicians who could mobilise the support of local personalities in return for patronage in metropolitan politics – rival *Sullani* such as Pompey, Crassus and the less well known Cornelius Cethegus. The last generation

Fig. 9 Denarius struck in 70 BC. The integration of Italian communities after the Social War is represented by the figures of Rome and Italy clasping hands in friendship – but we may note that it is Rome who has her foot on the globe, signifying world rule.

of the republic, as Cassius Dio was to put it, was to be a period of *dynasteia*, with a quite different political structure to what had gone before.

The distribution of power was also significantly changed by the exclusion of Marian supporters, and their sons, from politics. Sulla's reign of terror constituted a very significant disruption of the political system: the men who disappeared were not simply those who represented alternative sources of political or social influence to those who had seized power with Sulla, they also represented a considerable proportion of the experience and authority of the Senate. Even in areas such as foreign policy, where the second-century Senate had managed to provide a measure of continuity by reconciling the conflicting interests of its members, the dynasts would now increasingly simply use the Senate as a theatre for their struggles against one another. Far from making Sulla what he claimed to be, the restorer of senatorial authority, the effect of the proscriptions was to weaken that authority, insofar as one of the Senate's real bases was the political experience of its leading members. Sulla's constitutional reforms were not so much a restoration of senatorial authority to its pre-Gracchan position as an attempt to legitimate his own (unconstitutional) seizure of power. Pompey was to behave similarly in the late 50s, Caesar in the 40s and Augustus in the 20s.

In fact much of what Sulla did was innovatory; where he systematised aspects of Roman political procedure, that systematisation was itself something new, something transferred to Rome from Greek constitutional theory. Among the spoils Sulla brought back from the east were Aristotle's books, including the *Politics* (many years later, Cicero consulted them in Faustus Sulla's library). The new Senate represented the aristocracy of Greek political theory. Membership was no longer decided by the censors (the next censorship was not held until 70), but the automatic result of election to the twenty annual quaestorships. There were to be eight praetors and two consuls: eight plus two makes ten, the number of provinces, and the provinces were not to be governed by magistrates during their year of office (with the exception of the consuls, if required), but by ex-magistrates from the previous year. Far from being a return to the previous century, Sulla's Senate gave enormous opportunities to new men, whether from Latin equestrian families or leaders of the former allies. Its size was doubled to 600; and the effect of warfare, Marius' killings and Sulla's proscriptions was that perhaps two-thirds of its members came from families with no previous experience of senatorial procedure. Here again was a reason why the politics of the next generation was in the hands of those dynasts who could mobilise the support of Sulla's new senators.

On the other hand some of Sulla's rules were so artificial that they proved unworkable: most clearly, the attempt to eliminate potential trouble from tribunes by excluding them from subsequent election to any higher magistracy. If this harmed the ordinary citizens who looked to the tribunes for protection against abuses of magisterial power by lowering the standing of those who would be prepared to hold the office, it harmed young élite politicians a great deal more, by stopping them from winning popularity through their exercise of the office (the alternative was the much more expensive aedileship). Another issue which Sulla failed to solve was the composition of juries for the standing courts (*quaestiones*): Sulla brought the number of these up to seven, transferring the juries from equestrians to his enlarged and more easily controllable Senate.

Fig. 10 Bust of Sulla, his hair waving heroically like that of the young Alexander.

Chapter 6
Challenging Hortensius

These fifty-one member juries provided suitable audiences for Hortensius and Cicero on which to test their rhetorical expertise – particularly since so many of the respected speakers of the previous generation had died. New *patroni* were needed to represent before the Roman courts the interests of municipal families, especially those recently enfranchised and thus newly subject to, and unfamiliar with, the regulations of Roman law. It was during Sulla's dictatorship that Cicero made his first speech, the **Pro Quinctio**. The case concerns a dispute between Quinctius and Naevius, who had been his brother's business associate (and brother-in-law) and claimed possession of an estate in Gaul. Cicero follows Greek rhetorical rules very closely, and makes frequent use of commonplaces (*topoi*). In his introduction he makes the standard claim that he hasn't had time to prepare, and that he is outfaced by the brilliance of Hortensius. The *narratio* (account of the facts of the case) puts particular emphasis on describing the character of the actors (his client is a frugal rustic, his opponent a luxurious wastrel). Cicero may have spoken in other lawsuits during this period (*Pro Quinctio* 4 mentions four others), but it is the only one he chose to publish.

The extent to which civil conflict had resulted in social and economic as well as political disruption is illustrated by Cicero's next surviving speech, the **Pro Roscio Amerino**. This was delivered after Sulla had laid down his dictatorial office at the latest in 81, although he was still alive. The case is again about property. On the death of the elder Roscius, two powerful relatives in his home-town Ameria, Capito and Magnus, seized his property, assuming that they could ignore the son, who had been relegated to a rural estate by his father – normally a sign that a son would be disinherited. When the son caused trouble, and Ameria sent a delegation to Sulla on the son's behalf, they gave ten of Roscius' thirteen properties to Sulla's freedman Chrysogonus as a bribe, to make sure that the case would not be brought to Sulla's attention. They then accused the son of having his father murdered. In his speech for the defence, Cicero (who carefully avoids any mention of the will) turns the tables by depicting his opponents as wicked bandits and murderers

33

clearly acting without Sulla's authority. Sulla apparently made no attempt to protect his freedman, and the jury acquitted Roscius. Cicero could later represent the case as a blow for liberty against a tyrant – but that was in the context of the rule of Caesar and Mark Antony. We should rather see it as an attempt by some *Sullani*, especially members of the Metellan family, to control a freed slave who was exploiting his relationship with Sulla to the detriment of their own clients.

It was not therefore fear of Sulla that made Cicero go off to the East with his brother Quintus in 78/77, as suggested by Plutarch. Cicero's health may have been a factor: he seems to have been of a nervous disposition, and the tension of making forensic speeches was affecting him (*Brutus* 314). He would need to learn less strenuous techniques of delivery if he was not to exhaust himself. His interest in Greek philosophy may also have encouraged him to spend some time in Greece, in the context of his ambition to be a successful orator. Plutarch naturally overemphasises Cicero's own references to a stay at Athens, where he listened to the philosophical lectures of Antiochus of Ascalon. But even at Athens, lessons in rhetoric were as important to Cicero as in philosophy: he practised declamation with the Syrian Demetrius, a refugee from the collapse of the Seleucid monarchy. At Rhodes, he trained with Apollonius Molon, especially in order to develop voice control. It was perhaps from Apollonius that Cicero learnt of the theory of the three styles, and their appropriateness to the different functions of oratory: the plain style teaches, the middle style delights, and the grand style moves.

We know of a number of forensic appearances by Cicero on his return to Rome: e.g. a lost speech *Against Cluentius for Scamander*, and one appealing for the restoration of the property of a man from Thurii in southern Italy called M. Tullius (not necessarily a relative). Whether the speech **Pro Roscio Comoedo**, in which he successfully opposed Hortensius, dates to this period or to c. 66 is disputed; in any case Hortensius continued to be recognised as Rome's most authoritative orator until 70.

Cicero now had sufficient public status to be elected to his first public office, the quaestorship, in 75. Throughout the 70s Sullan generals were competing for prestige by fighting the enemies of the regime, rather than each other: Metellus Pius and Pompey in Spain fighting Sertorius, Lucullus in Africa (76-75) and in the East fighting Mithridates (from 73 on). What threatened stability was an acute financial crisis brought about directly by the extension of citizenship to all Italians. The financing of the entire army, and not just the 40% who had hitherto been Roman citizens, was now the responsibility of the Roman treasury. While the newly enfranchised communities of Italy suddenly enjoyed an enormous increase in wealth (much of which was used on public building programmes), the Roman treasury had no new sources of income. Pompey in Nearer Spain was constantly short of supplies (Metellus Pius in Further Spain was in a better position, since his province produced a considerable amount of gold and silver). It was Lucullus as consul in 74 who turned his attention to finance and found the money for Pompey in Spain. Later he went on to reform the tax-collecting procedures in the eastern provinces. Although that resulted in great unpopularity with the Romans who collected these taxes and was a factor in Lucullus' recall in 67, it laid the foundations for a solution to the treasury's shortfall. Subsequently Pompey's conquests in the East, and then Caesar's in Gaul, greatly increased the tax base from which the Roman government derived its revenue. But in the 70s there were problems even in buying enough grain to feed the urban population of Rome: that was the context in which Cicero served as quaestor in western Sicily, where he managed to increase the supply of grain to Rome by cutting out the traditional back-handers paid to the collecting officials.

Cicero's performance as quaestor clearly won him friends at Rome, as well as amongst the taxpayers of Sicily. But a passage in his later philosophical dialogue the *Tusculan Disputations* shows how he also used his stay on the island to exploit his intellectual capital. The superiority brought by scholarship could be used to impress provincials as well as metropolitan Romans:

> When I was quaestor in Sicily I succeeded in locating the grave of Archimedes, which was unknown to the Syracusans.... So one of the most illustrious cities in the Greek world would have remained completely ignorant of the tomb of its most brilliant citizen, if a man from Arpinum had not come and shown it to them.
>
> (*Tusculans* 5, 23.64)

While Pompey, Metellus Pius and Lucullus sought to compete with one another through military expeditions, other *Sullani* remained at Rome, and improved their position through the exercise of patronage. Foremost among them was Marcus Crassus. Crassus made a point of assisting the new senators with political advice, and more concretely by supplying them with refurbished houses and hiring out high-status flats to them. For Crassus in particular, the imminent return of Pompey from Spain after his elimination of Sertorius (the last surviving supporter of the pre-Sullan regime) posed a threat: he needed to find some military glory to balance Pompey's. The answer to his prayers came in the form of a slave-rebellion led by Spartacus, which thanks to the incompetence of one of the consuls of 73, Cassius Longinus, and those of 72, Cn. Cornelius Lentulus Clodianus and L. Gellius Publicola (both supporters of Pompey), could be represented as a major threat to public order. Crassus raised an army at his own expense, and found opportunity to fight several separate battles against different groups of insurgent slaves. After his final victory, he crucified several thousand of Spartacus' followers along the Via Appia. Crassus' motives in all this were not so much those of a leading Roman slave-owner (as some used to think), but rather those of a Roman politician seeking enough military glory to be able to face his rival on equal terms – and indeed Pompey agreed to share the consulship for 70 with Crassus.

That did not mean they had a common political agenda, and it is pointless to see them as following either pro- or anti-Sullan policies. One of the unworkable elements in Sulla's constitution, the ban on office-holding by ex-tribunes, had been lifted by the ('Sullan') C. Aurelius Cotta in 75. In 70, his brother L. Cotta proposed to remove the issue of who provided the juries through a compromise which shared jury-service equally between three panels of senators, equestrians, and a slightly less wealthy status-group known as the *tribuni aerarii*. On one interpretation, the issue became a trial of strength between Pompey and the other *Sullani* who had controlled metropolitan politics in the previous years, especially members of the Metellan family.

That was the context of the **Verrine Orations** which were to enable Cicero to replace Hortensius as the leading orator at Rome. C. Verres had been one of those who joined Sulla on his return to Italy in 83 (taking Carbo's treasure-chest with him), and was close to the Metelli. Following his praetorship in 74, he governed Sicily for three years. Here he made the mistake of alienating an extremely powerful provincial magnate, Sthenius of Thermae (Termini Himerese), who fled to Rome to avoid sentencing by Verres' court. Cicero had done business with Sthenius during his quaestorship, and had an obligation to defend him. Apart from indignation at what Verres had done, he no doubt also thought of the advantages that Sicilian support in the shape of grain and money might bring him in the following year (69) when he was to hold the expensive office of aedile. Cicero was backed by the Marcelli, hereditary patrons of Sicily since their ancestor had destroyed the kingdom of Syracuse in 212. Against him stood Hortensius and the Metelli, but not Pompey: on the contrary, the prosecution of Verres suited Pompey very well. He wanted to represent himself as supporting

Cotta's reforms, and would gain either way. If Cicero persuaded the jury, Pompey's opponents would be humiliated; if Verres was acquitted, Pompey would be able to claim that a senatorial jury was clearly biased, and that the courts should be taken away from senatorial control. (Not all scholars agree that Pompey had an interest in Verres' trial.)

The first of the Verrine speeches is the **Divinatio in Q. Caecilium**: as published, it is a rhetorical essay summarising the background to the case, as though it had been presented at an initial hearing in which Cicero persuaded the court that he, and not Verres' former quaestor Caecilius, had the right to prosecute. Cicero was given permission to proceed, and to spend 110 days collecting evidence in Sicily; the governor (L. Metellus) tried to make things difficult for him, and another case was brought before the extortion court with the intention of preventing Verres' case from being heard until the following year, when Hortensius and Lucius' brother Q. Metellus Creticus would be consuls and a third brother M. Metellus would be the praetor presiding over the extortion court. But Cicero acted quickly, and the mass of evidence which he was able to marshal in the *Actio Prima* made Verres go into voluntary exile at Massilia (Marseille) without waiting to be formally condemned. Cicero was able to demonstrate that, amongst other crimes, Verres had plundered property to the value of forty million sesterces. The court ordered the Sicilians to be reimbursed to the extent of three million. There was no need for the customary second presentation of evidence, the *Actio Secunda*. This series of speeches was never delivered, but consists of a series of five essays on the same theme, dealing at length with categories of material as specified in rhetorical handbooks on *inventio*: the accused's earlier career, and the four classes of crimes he committed (corresponding to the cardinal virtues in a panegyric), e.g. temple-plundering, abuses of judicial power and military failure. The *Actio Secunda* contains many passages famous for their sensational and florid rhetoric, including Verres' parties on the beach near Syracuse and his crucifixion of a Roman citizen. In all this the historian has to distinguish between what was spoken at the trial, and the text as Cicero later had it published, for a separate purpose – to ensure that everyone who could read Latin knew that he had replaced Hortensius as Rome's foremost orator.

Chapter 7
To the Top of the Ladder

Although a jury of senators had been prepared to condemn Verres, Cotta's compromise reform of the jury panels was accepted. Cicero's success had been an important contribution to strengthening Pompey's primacy, and hence both the Metelli and Crassus remained suspicious of Cicero thereafter. In 69, as aedile, Cicero exploited the gratitude of Sthenius and other Sicilians by importing enough low-cost corn to be able to lower the price at Rome, in spite of the major dislocation which Mediterranean shipping was suffering in this period at the hands of Cilician pirates. This was a problem which Pompey subsequently exploited in 67 when the *Lex Gabinia* awarded him special powers of command to clear the seas – a precedent for later legislation enabling particular commanders (Pompey, Caesar, and later the emperors) to exercise military power equal to that exercised by ordinary pro-magistrates, and for a longer term. The fact that Pompey achieved his military aims against the pirates within three months shows the potential of Roman power, once a particular Roman politician had succeeded in mobilising that power.

Before that, Cicero made some other speeches which survive. Two of them were before the extortion court: the *Pro Fonteio* and the *Pro Oppio*. In the **Pro Fonteio**, Cicero shows that he can marshal all the arguments that Hortensius might have used for the defence in Verres' trial. Just as Cicero had denigrated Verres' military ability in *In Verrem* 5, so now he extols that of Fonteius. While Cicero had represented the Sicilian provincials (on his own side) as aristocrats of the highest integrity, the Gauls who accuse Fonteius were perjurers and traditional enemies of Rome, barbarians who were trying to destroy a Roman of high status. It was the jury's duty to protect him (§§ 46-9).

In 69 or 68, Cicero also made an important and complex speech in defence of Caecina, a member of the ruling clan in the Etruscan city of Volaterrae. Cicero later referred to the **Pro Caecina** in the *Orator* (§ 102) as the most successful of his speeches in the plain style, since much of the argument hinged on the interpretation of legal terminology. Cicero was unable to prove his client's entitlement to the ownership of a particular estate at Tarquinia, bequeathed to him by his wife Caesennia, who had bought it from a relative of her former husband through an agent, Aebutius, who now refused to give up possession. Instead, Cicero arranged his speech around a number of peripheral if not irrelevant issues, such as whether a citizen of Volaterrae (deprived of civic rights by Sulla) could legally inherit under Roman law, and in particular whether it had been appropriate for Caecina to further his claim by seeking an interdict from the praetor under a law against violence. This particular issue, as has been brilliantly demonstrated by the American historian Bruce Frier, shows how Cicero was prepared to ignore an

Fig. 11 The first-century sarcophagus of Caecina Selcia, one of the Caecinae of Volaterrae, illustrates the survival of Etruscan culture into the period when all Italians had become Roman citizens.

established procedure of Roman law to an extent that leaves the audience (and the modern reader) entirely unaware that what he described as an act of unprovoked violence was actually a legitimate, if archaic, procedure by which two litigants clarified which of them was to be the plaintiff and which the accused. Cicero makes no bones about his preference for 'equity' over a strict interpretation of legal procedure, appealing to the precedent of Crassus' speech for Curio (§ 53f., 67ff.; see p. 19 above). In the *Pro Caecina*, Cicero was in fact not so much liberalising a legal procedure, as ignoring it completely.

Other speeches from this period were lost or never published; in 66 came Cicero's longest speech, the **Pro Cluentio**. Cluentius was accused under two different provisions of the Sullan law against murder, for having first tried to dispose of his step-father Oppianicus by bribing a jury to convict him of murder, and when that failed, for having tried to poison him. Cicero manages to depict Cluentius' opponents, including his own mother Sassia, in the worst possible light. The artificial contrast leaves the listener with the feeling that Cluentius must be innocent – or at any rate more innocent than his accusers. Another artificial contrast Cicero uses in this speech is between his client, who is so honest that he only wants strictly legal arguments to be used, and the *patronus*, Cicero himself, who wants to win the case by using wider arguments (which he certainly does, representing the accusations of bribery as proof that Oppianicus wanted to overthrow the entire state). According to Quintilian, Cicero boasted that he had brought down a fog on the eyes of the jury (*Institutio Oratoria* 2, 17.21; cf. 11, 1.61ff.).

In 66, Cicero held the praetorship, making his first speech on a political rather than forensic subject: the proposal that Pompey, fresh from his success over the pirates, should be granted exceptional powers to take over from Lucullus the war which the latter had been fighting with some success against Mithridates. In this speech, known variously as the **De Imperio Cn. Pompeii** or as the **Pro Lege Manilia**, Cicero exploits Greek rules of panegyric, extolling the incomparable bravery, experience, and good fortune of Pompey. It begins with an appeal for sympathy (*captatio benevolentiae*) suggesting that because he had not addressed a political assembly (*contio*) before, he deserved the goodwill due to an inexperienced speaker. There are parallels from Greek literature (Mithridates is compared to Medea, § 22). But the speech is far from a theoretical school exercise: it also makes allowances for the realities of Roman political power. It contains a typically Roman concern with the *auctoritas* both of the proposal's opponents and of its supporters (§§17/50-23/68).

Cicero made other speeches to the populace in 66, including one (not preserved) on Sulla's treasure chest, and forensic speeches *Pro Q. Gallio*, *Pro Fundanio* (dealing with electoral bribery) and *Pro C. Cornelio*.

Pompey's absence in the East allowed Crassus to re-emerge at the centre of the political stage. Although he held the censorship in 65 BC, he failed to exclude his opponents from the Senate, he failed in a first attempt to annex Egypt, and he failed to have his supporters elected to magistracies. One of those he backed was L. Sergius Catilina, who had been unable to stand for the consulate in the elections of 66 because he was accused of corruption during his governorship of Africa; the suggestion that he tried to seize power by violence in late 66 (the so-called 'First Catilinarian Conspiracy') is likely to have been an invention of his opponents. He stood again in the electoral campaign of 64; his opponents – or Crassus – were so unwilling to see him elected that they gave their support to Cicero and to C. Antonius Hybrida, one of the sons of the orator (see p. 16 above). A speech in which Cicero attacked his competitors Catiline and Antonius, the *In Toga Candida*, no longer survives, though a commentary on it written by Asconius in the first century AD does survive. We also have the **Commentariolum Petitionis**, a short essay ascribed to Cicero's brother Quintus listing the different groups of voters whose support is needed by a candidate. Whoever wrote it, it describes the electoral atmosphere of the late republic, and is unlikely to have been written much later. (It contains no reference to the 'first' conspiracy of Catiline, but that is hardly surprising if that conspiracy was a fiction of Catiline's opponents.)

Chapter 8
Cicero's Year

Cicero's election as consul, as a 'new man' (*novus homo*) without consular or even praetorian ancestors, at the earliest age allowed by law, and with the support of every single electoral unit in the centuriate assembly, was a tremendous achievement. It demonstrated how effective Cicero's judicious use of his rhetorical skills had been in winning the support both of rival members of the Sullan establishment, and of the leaders of municipalities throughout Italy whom the Social War and Sulla's reforms were introducing into the Roman political network, a century after Arpinum itself had begun to become part of the Roman community. Cicero's efforts as aedile to use his Sicilian connections to provide grain for ordinary Romans also paid off.

Cicero's consulship brought him the public status he had craved. In the autumn of 63, Catiline made an attempt – a real one, this time – to seize power; Cicero had the good fortune to organise the suppression of the conspiracy. A few years later, in order to ensure that this political achievement would never be forgotten, he published a collection of the four major speeches he had made against Catiline, along with eight other speeches from his consular year. These speeches were edited: what went into them was what was relevant to the political issues of 60 BC. In particular Cicero wished to defend his decision as consul to override the clear civic rights of the conspirators in having them executed without trial by emphasising in these later publications a senatorial recommendation, the *Senatus Consultum Ultimum* ('SCU' or 'Last Decree') which the Senate had passed in October (that the SCU had actually made any difference at the time when the conspirators were executed in December is most unlikely). The leading role Cicero naturally assigned himself in these speeches is probably sufficient explanation why Sallust, when he came to write his history of the conspiracy twenty years later, felt able to minimise their role: everyone who read Latin already knew them. Sallust was also a writer who was more interested in highlighting conflict; and by ignoring Cicero he was able to focus his reader's attention on the contrasting characteristics of Caesar (who had opposed the death penalty) and Cato (who had supported it).

Fig. 12 This first-century statue of a public speaker (now at Florence) shows the respect awarded to oratory during the Ciceronian period.

The year began with two speeches **De Lege Agraria contra Rullum.** They opposed a land law proposed by the tribune Rullus – an attempt by Julius Caesar or others, perhaps including Crassus, to appoint commissioners who would have semi-permanent authority within Italy which might rival that of Pompey, soon to return from his eastern conquests. Cicero's speeches on this subject to the Senate are less ornamental than those to the people.

The next speech in the collection is the **Pro Rabirio perduellionis reo**. Rabirius was accused of involvement in the killing of Saturninus in 100 BC (see p. 18 above). In 63, he was prosecuted by an antiquated procedure before the *comitia centuriata*, for motives that were political – the case threatened to reopen conflict between the 'Marians' (Caesar, perhaps Crassus) and those who upheld senatorial authority, like Cicero. Later in 63 Cicero was to interpret the SCU as overriding established law; those responsible for Saturninus' death also claimed that they had acted in accordance with such a senatorial decree. The speech as published is clearly a defence of that position. Cicero uses the grand style, as was appropriate in a lawsuit that was really a political demonstration. Both sides argued in their speeches that the stability of the entire *res publica* was threatened by their opponents. Once again we find Cicero arguing against strict constitutionalism, both regarding the legal protection due to a citizen's life, and the archaic (but undoubtedly legal) procedures selected by the prosecution.

In the late republic, the SCU was little more than a fig-leaf which those who could muster a majority in the Senate used to legitimate the use of force. But force played a much greater role in Roman life than in modern societies, and the protection offered by statute law was much more restricted. Cicero was also able to marshal historical *exempla* illustrating the view that those caught actually committing a crime (*in flagrante*) could be summarily executed; that was a standard position in Roman criminal law. He also argued that by organising a treasonous conspiracy, Catiline and his supporters had become public enemies (*hostes*), thereby forfeiting the protection with which the law privileged Roman citizens. Nevertheless Cicero's willingness simply to ignore clear legal provisions of statute law should make us hesitate to assume that he was above the political gangsterism of his time. The lack of clarity about the primacy of law meant that what one side saw as a legal execution, their political opponents could describe as butchery: a good example is the description of Catiline executing Sullan opponents in the *Commentariolum Petitionis* (§ 45).

The four **Catilinarians** allow us to identify the slight differences in approach that Cicero used in speeches to different audiences. There is a striking religious element in the conclusion of the *Third Catilinarian*, absent from any of Cicero's speeches to the Senate, perhaps because it was addressed to the people. Again, we should remember that what we actually have are published revisions. Thus the text of the *First Catilinarian* should be read not just as a speech recited on November 8th, 63: it was also a justification composed a couple of years later of Cicero's view of how great the danger had been from the start. It was re-written in the form of a judicial speech. The *Fourth Catilinarian* is possibly a conflation of two separate speeches in the Senate. Cicero avoids mentioning the SCU, and again represents the speech as an inquisition before the Senate of individuals whose opposition (i.e. to Cicero) had made them forfeit their civic rights.

The other major speech Cicero made as consul was the **Pro Murena**. Cicero had seen in the summer of 63 that it was imperative for reliable anti-Catilinarian consuls to be elected and in post to suppress the military uprising that in fact occurred later in the year. Catiline made a last attempt to win the consulship constitutionally, and his opponents successfully used bribery against him. This led to the opposition of Cato, a young senator who hoped to buttress his authority by standing up for strict morality in the tradition of his famous great-grandfather, Cato the Censor. In November (in between the *Second* and the *Third Catilinarian*), Cato prosecuted Murena for electoral malpractice (he did not, however, prosecute the other successful candidate Junius Silanus, who just happened to be his brother-in-law). He was joined by Cicero's old friend the jurist Servius Sulpicius Rufus, who had failed to win election against Murena in spite of Cicero's own support for him.

The humour of the *Pro Murena* makes it one of Cicero's most enjoyable speeches: Plutarch says he had been up all night preparing it (*Cicero* 53.3). Pliny tells us that the published version was revised and shortened (*Letters* 1, 20.7). Thus § 57 has a heading referring to two further charges brought by the other prosecutors, Postumius and Servius, suggesting that in publishing this speech Cicero was mainly interested in its literary qualities, i.e. the humorous onslaught against Cato and Servius Sulpicius, who had to represent themselves as (philosophically and legally) sticklers for the law. The speech is another instance of Cicero managing to deny the clear truth of the charges, and marginalising Cato and Sulpicius through humour without permanently alienating them. Cicero ridicules the claim that Sulpicius deserved election because of his legal expertise: he makes fun of the arcane formulae of Roman legal procedure, and asserts that the whole of Roman law can be learnt in three days (§ 28). But there was also a serious issue in the case, as the peroration suggests: Cicero evokes the all-too-real memories of political assassination and civil war in the recent past to underline the importance of having legitimately elected magistrates ready to enter office in January 62.

If Catiline's conspiracy was built up by Cicero, it was nevertheless a real threat to stability. Catiline was a political actor in his own right;

he had also been built up by Crassus, perhaps as a counterweight to Pompey, perhaps to give Crassus himself an excuse for leading military operations against a rebellion as he had done against Spartacus eight years before. Pompey too would have been happy for an excuse to conduct military operations against Catiline within marching distance of Rome. By acting decisively to eliminate Catiline, Cicero had prevented Crassus and Pompey from exploiting the situation to seize power for themselves, and had thus saved Rome from the danger of a very serious civil war on the return of Pompey and his army from the East.

Cicero's success in arranging for the rebellion to be suppressed by his consular colleague Antonius was not to Pompey's liking, and he was markedly cool towards Cicero on his return to Rome in 62. When Crassus greeted Pompey in the Senate with a florid speech extolling Cicero's services in saving the republic, he was more interested in needling Pompey than doing Cicero a favour.

Cicero's political position when he laid down his consulship was far from secure. Although he had managed to have his brother Quintus elected as one of the praetors for the following year, he had made more enemies than friends, and he had good reason to fear the kind of prosecution which faced many another magistrate at the end of his period of office. Most of the Metelli had been hostile ever since the Verres trial: Caecilius Metellus Nepos, tribune in 63/62, even prevented Cicero from making the customary resignation speech. Another important family he had permanently alienated was that of Julia, widow of Lentulus Sura (cos. 71), one of the executed conspirators, and her three sons (by a previous marriage). One of them was Mark Antony.

Chapter 9
Exclusion and Exile

After his consulship Cicero was therefore in no position to relax. Speech after speech was needed to reinforce his own authority, and the esteem conferred by acquaintance with Greek culture. In the **Pro Sulla**, he defended Pompey's brother-in-law on a charge of being involved in Catiline's conspiracy; Sulla had just happened to lend Cicero 2,000,000 sesterces to buy a house on the Palatine from Crassus (Aulus Gellius 12, 12.2). Cicero selected the grand style for this speech, basing the argument on the fact that since he had dealt with Catiline, he knew authoritatively who had, and who had not, been involved.

In another speech, **Pro Archia Poeta**, he defended a claim by a poet from Syria to have been granted Roman citizenship by being entered on the civic register of the municipality of Heraclea in Lucania in Greek-speaking southern Italy. Archias had received this privilege through the patronage of Lucullus (in whose honour he had written an epic), and the accusation that it was not valid came from Lucullus' enemies, the supporters of Pompey. In his speech, Cicero naturally enough concentrates on the value of culture and scholarship, and implicitly downgrades the importance of other virtues: in particular the military ability that had made Pompey great. Other speeches from this period were not published or were lost, like the *In Clodium et Curionem*.

The publication of these and other speeches during the years after his consulship was necessary if Cicero was to give his momentary achievement permanence. He also wrote narrative accounts of the events of his consulship (*commentarii*) in both Greek and Latin, and an epic poem on the same theme. This was hardly megalomania (as was already suggested in antiquity, for instance in the Pseudo-Sallustian invectives against Cicero). It was essentially the same strategy as that pursued by other Roman ex-magistrates who sought to give permanence to their conquests or their liberality through monuments, coins, paintings and mosaics (e.g. those representing the gladiatorial games they had put on). If Cicero did not have the occasion for public building, he could write. The collection of twelve consular speeches (*orationes consulares*: *Ad Att.* 2, 1.3) should be seen in this light. They comprised the two speeches on Rullus' agrarian law, *de Othone, Pro Rabirio*, a speech on the sons of the proscribed, the speech Metellus Nepos prevented him from giving at his resignation, four Catilinarians, and two shorter speeches on agrarian issues.

The need to remain in the public eye became all the more urgent with the creation of the political understanding between Pompey, Crassus and Caesar, over-formally known as the 'First Triumvirate'. Pompey had found it impossible to persuade the Roman establishment either to approve his settlement of the eastern territories he had conquered, or to provide the land in Italy with which he had promised to reward his victorious soldiers. Caesar exploited the alliance to win the consulship for 59, and his daughter became Pompey's fourth wife. Cicero realised that the triumvirate threatened to marginalise all other political actors. In 59, supporters of Pompey and Crassus prosecuted Flaccus, who as praetor in 63 had assisted Cicero by arresting a group of Catiline's supporters at the Milvian bridge outside Rome. He was accused of extortion as governor of Asia, and Cicero successfully defended him in the **Pro Flacco.**

Worse was to come, in the person of Publius Clodius Pulcher. Clodius' family was an ancient one, with a radical tradition in politics. (Clodius was simply a popular spelling of Claudius.) His grandfather had been consul (in 143), censor and *princeps senatus*, had married his daughter to Tiberius Gracchus, and had been one of the three Gracchan land commissioners. His father had been consul in 79 as a supporter of Sulla. Unfortunately he died as governor of Macedonia in 76, leaving three daughters and three sons in straitened circumstances, with all the expense of providing a dowry and investing in a political career. The eldest daughter had married Q. Marcius Rex (cos. 68); the second married Q. Metellus Celer, who had given Cicero all necessary support in 63, while Celer's brother Nepos was an open enemy. (Metellus died in 59, and this Clodia led an independent life thereafter; the 'Lesbia' of Catullus' poetry is generally supposed to be based on her.) The youngest daughter had been married for a time to Lucullus; the divorce, in 66, was not amicable, and Lucullus prosecuted her for incest with her brother Clodius. Of the sons, the elder, Appius Claudius Pulcher, was to become praetor in 57, and consul in 54 and the second, Gaius, praetor in 56. The youngest son, Publius Clodius, did not have the patience to wait until he became a political force through the regular magisterial ladder. In the Gracchan tradition, he sought to win power by mobilising sections of the urban population as a tribune. He managed to articulate some of the grievances of ordinary Roman craftsmen and shopkeepers, possibly exacerbated by the failure of the new Italian senators to patronise them in the way to which they had become accustomed. This made him both a potential ally, and a rival, to Caesar, who himself claimed to represent the popular political line of Marius, who had been married to Caesar's aunt.

Fig. 13 Denarius of 113 or 112 BC, showing voting by secret ballot at a Roman assembly. (For the introduction of the secret ballot at Arpinum, see p. 15.) Although Roman politics were far from 'democratic', the power of the assembly could be mobilised by tribunes who articulated the wishes of sections of the urban electorate.

In 63, Caesar had been elected *Pontifex Maximus*, head of the board of experts in religious law. On the night of December 4th to 5th in the following year, the festival of the *Bona Dea* was held in his house, under the presidency of his wife Pompeia. This was a nocturnal religious ceremony at which only women of patrician family were supposed to be present. Clodius sought to discredit Caesar by entering the house as though he was Pompeia's lover (his exact motives are uncertain, since our only contemporary source is actually Cicero). Caesar found it necessary to divorce Pompeia, and Clodius stood trial the following year; he was acquitted, even though Cicero had disproved his alibi. Clodius did not forget Cicero's hostility. When he was consul in 59, Caesar thought that notwithstanding the *Bona Dea* scandal, Clodius would be a potential supporter while he himself was outside Rome as governor of Gaul; he engineered Clodius' (legally dubious) adoption into a plebeian family, so that he could stand for the tribunate of 59/58.

Early in 58, Clodius passed a measure outlawing those who had executed citizens without trial: it was so clearly aimed at Cicero that

Cicero was later able to argue that it was framed for him alone, and therefore illegal. Cicero saw that he would receive no support from the two consuls, Gabinius and Piso, and instead of waiting for a formal trial he left Rome in March 58, hoping that this would force Clodius' opponents in the Senate to rally to Cicero's side and recall him at once. In the meantime he intended to wait in southern Italy or Sicily. Instead, Clodius had a specific law passed declaring Cicero an exile who was to be denied fire and water within four hundred miles of Rome, effectively forcing him to leave Italy for Greece.

As tribune, Clodius constructed a power-base in his own right, using well-organised groups of supporters to control the legislative and electoral assemblies of the metropolis. This made him too powerful both for Caesar (who wanted to be the unchallenged patron of the *populus*) and for Pompey, who needed to control the assemblies. Clodius tried to play the two off against each other: in his speeches he accused Pompey of being more besotted with Caesar's daughter than behoved a Roman husband, and – at the same time – of being a homosexual effeminate. He also questioned the validity of some of Caesar's legislation.

Pompey calculated that Cicero had now realised how limited his power was; if he was recalled, he would have no choice but to behave with appropriate gratitude to those who had saved him, and accept the primacy of the triumvirate. One of the consuls of 57 BC, P. Cornelius Lentulus Spinther, arranged for the Senate to recall him.

For about a year following his return to Rome on September 4th, 57, Cicero hoped he could continue to act as an independent political figure. It was essential that he should represent his recall as a victory for constitutional politics rather than a favour granted by Pompey. To this end he published a group of seven **Post Reditum** speeches. The collection contains two speeches of thanks following his return. Before his competitors in the Senate he suggests that his return is a return to legality for the entire state, while to the people he represents it as a personal victory over his opponents, particularly Clodius. The attack on Clodius is carried further in **De domo sua ad pontifices** (*To the Priests regarding his House*), and in a speech **De haruspicum responso** (*Regarding the Soothsayers' Opinion*) given in the following year. Both of these speeches draw our attention to the wider issue of the manipulation of religious rituals for political advantage, though that practice was by no means an innovation of the late republic.

The 'post reditum' speeches also include two forensic speeches delivered in 56, the **Pro Sestio** and the **Pro Caelio**. Sestius had been a tribune in 57, supporting Cicero's return from exile, and accordingly was prosecuted for violence by Clodius after his term of office had come to an end. But Clodius no longer had any allies, not even the absent Caesar. The support of Pompey (as a witness) and speeches by Crassus and Hortensius as well as Cicero resulted in Sestius' acquittal. Cicero's theme in the *Pro Sestio* is that of political concord between the different social orders. In the published speech, Clodius' attack on Sestius is seen very much as an attack on Cicero himself (half of it, §§ 15-71, is largely about Cicero's exile): the political background of the triumvirate is completely lost sight of. Another speech, the **In Vatinium**, was part of the procedure of Sestius' trial (the cross-examination of a hostile witness).

56 was also the year of the **Pro Caelio**, one of the most successful of Cicero's literary pieces, and a school text for centuries, with dubious consequences for the acceptance of double standards in matters of sexual morality. Again Cicero found himself alongside Crassus and attacking Clodius, this time through his sister, the widow of Metellus Celer. This vicious, but immensely lively and imaginative, attack on Clodia (who was simply one of the witnesses brought forward by the prosecution) has the function of distracting the reader, and the jury, from the real charges (which at the trial were dealt with by Crassus and Caelius himself) – that Caelius was involved in a plot to have the Alexandrian ambassador Dio killed on the instructions of, or at least to the advantage of, the exiled King Ptolemy XII Auletes of Egypt, who was staying with Pompey.

We know from other sources that the possibility of Roman military intervention to restore Ptolemy to his throne against the opposition of the Alexandrians was a major political issue in these years; Ptolemy is reported to have offered Caesar a bribe of 10,000,000 sesterces for his support in 59. Whichever Roman commander won the appointment would also be able to tap the wealth of Egypt, the last major hellenistic kingdom. Pompey, Crassus, and Cicero's supporter Lentulus Spinther (now governor of Cilicia) all had a claim to be allowed to suppress Alexandrian opposition to Ptolemy. On the other hand a majority of senators had no wish for such an expedition to take place, if it would merely strengthen the position of one or other of their powerful competitors. In the *Pro Caelio*, Cicero manages to keep the jury in the dark about the political background, and represents the charges as due to a woman as immoral as her brother seeking vengeance against a former lover.

Cicero was wrong if he thought that Caesar could be separated from Pompey and Crassus, as Clodius now was. Attempts to have some of Caesar's legislation rescinded were not supported by the Senate, and

– like the independent political line which Clodius was taking – had the opposite effect of galvanising Caesar to restore the triumvirate at the so-called Conference of Luca (in fact there was no such conference, just meetings between Caesar and Crassus at Ravenna, and with Pompey at Luca). Crassus and Pompey were in a strong position, and Caesar had to agree to a second consulship for them in 55; what he got in return was another five-year period as governor of Gaul. With Pompey and Crassus as consuls, it was imperative that Caesar should gain some additional glory for himself. In 55 BC, he led two minor expeditions across the Rhine and across the English Channel in order to be able to claim to Italian public opinion that, following the pacification of Gaul, he was now going on to conquer new territory.

Chapter 10
The Dynasts in Control

The restoration of the triumvirate had the effect of creating a source of authority which could override the annual magistrates. It was no longer possible for office-holders, even if they did not actually owe their election to the dynasts, to go against their will following open discussion in the Senate or at a popular *contio*, as Pompey's competitors had done in the 70s and 60s.

The consuls elected each year were excluded from campaigning or waging war, excluded by the power of these three men (Appian, BC 2, 3.19: ὅτι τε ἀνὰ ἔτος ἕκαστον ὕπατοι στρατεύειν μέν που καὶ πολεμεῖν ἀπεγίνωσκον, διακλειόμενοι τῇ δυναστείᾳ τῶνδε τῶν τριῶν ἀνδρῶν).

After his return to Rome in 57, Cicero had thought that he could associate himself with Crassus and Pompey, and alienate them from Clodius and Caesar; now he realised that he had to obey all three if he was not to be excluded from public life altogether (*Ad Fam.* 1, 9.9).

Already in 56 Cicero found himself forced to appear for Caesar's supporter L. Cornelius Balbus (who came from Gades in Spain, and was responsible for organising the supplies for Caesar's army) in the **Pro Balbo**, a speech defending his right to Roman citizenship. He was also required to argue the case for selecting Macedonia and Syria as the two provinces due to be assigned to the consuls for the following year, and for leaving Gaul in Caesar's hands (**De Provinciis Consularibus**).

In November 55, Cicero responded to the suppression of open decision-making by composing a treatise on oratory in three books whose theme was precisely the primacy of public political discourse: the **De Oratore** (cf. *Ad Att.* 4, 5). It was in the form of a dialogue, the dramatic date of which was September 91 BC, set on the orator Crassus' estate at Tusculum just before his death. A minor character is Aurelius Cotta, whom Cicero claims as his source. In the introduction, Crassus puts the case for the central role of oratory. In Book 1, he is criticised by Scaevola the Augur and Antonius, who respectively argue for the primacy of 'wisdom' over oratory, and suggest that the ideal of the perfect orator is unattainable. Crassus responds to Antonius' restricted view of the orator as nothing more than a technically competent public speaker. We recall that the historical Antonius' unprincipled use of rhetorical techniques meant that his speeches were so full of falsehoods and contradictions that he could not publish them. Cicero had no such fears about his own speeches: he clearly wanted the reader to recognise Crassus' ideal orator in Cicero himself.

In Book 2, Antonius expounds a number of technical points, and discusses how rhetorical expertise might improve other forms of literature e.g. historiography. He is also made a proponent of Cicero's ideas (a development of Greek theory) about the three functions of oratory (*delectare, probare, movere*: to give pleasure, to prove, and to mobilise the emotions). Not surprisingly, Antonius suggests that those aspects on which Cicero himself put the most emphasis were the skills which really mattered. In Book 3, Crassus talks about presentation, in particular *elocutio* and *pronuntiatio* (expression and delivery). He also repeats the point that the orator needs to be philosophically trained. Cicero is trying to overcome a long tradition of opposition between philosophy and rhetoric which went back to the writings of Plato and the sophists. Even some Roman philhellenes like Hortensius remained unpersuaded by Cicero's argument that the philosophy in which he had special expertise was relevant to Rome (*De Finibus* 1, 1.2).

If Cicero claimed to be both Rome's greatest expert on Greek philosophy and her most successful public speaker, he was now forced to put those skills at the disposal of others. Only in his writings was he free: he was able to attack Caesar's father-in-law, Calpurnius Piso, whom he blamed for failing as consul in 58 to prevent his exile. Even if he had wanted to, Cicero was not allowed to prosecute him for corruption on his return as governor of Macedonia in 56. Instead, he denigrated Piso for all eternity by writing his most famous invective, the **In Pisonem**.

But even in his writings, such as the epic poem *De Temporibus Suis*, he had to recognise that the political world had become post-republican. One response was to re-locate open, republican government in an ideal world. In 54, he began his **De Re Publica**, the *Commonwealth* or *Republic*. It is an account of a discussion said to have taken place shortly before the death of the younger Scipio in 129 BC, which Cicero claims to have heard about from Rutilius Rufus, whom he had visited in exile in Smyrna in 78/77. Like Plato's dialogue of the same name, it takes place in an earlier world before the writers' respective communities (Athens and Rome) had come to grief through external war and civil conflict. The dialogue incidentally describes the Stoic idea of a world community sharing universal ideas of justice, i.e. Natural Law.

It is not right to set aside this law, nor is it permitted to restrict it in any detail, nor can it be totally abolished, nor can we be freed from this law either through the Senate or through the people, nor is any Sextus Aelius required as its expert interpreter, nor will this law be one at Rome, another at Athens, one now, another in the future, but a single law, eternal and immutable, will bind all peoples at all times.

(3, 22/33)

In this remarkable dialogue, Cicero argues for a source of authority (of which, notwithstanding his comment about the famous jurist Aelius Catus, cos. 198 BC, Cicero himself was the interpreter) beyond the reach of the legislative institutions of Rome, which were all now under the control of the dynasts. To add to the authority of that ideal source of law, he ascribed his exposition to an equally ideal 'Scipionic circle' (see p. 21 above). In late antiquity, the emphasis on a divinely guaranteed Natural Law attracted both pagan and Christian intellectuals, and although most of the dialogue was lost until fragments were found by Cardinal Angelo Mai in 1822, the final section, known as the **Somnium Scipionis**, survived through the Middle Ages because of a commentary by the fifth-century pagan scholar Macrobius. This 'Dream of Scipio' describes a vision which the conqueror of Hannibal is supposed to have had just before his death, a vision in which he realised just how relatively unimportant were military glory and political success (both his own and, more remarkably, that of the Roman state) in the context of eternity.

Whether or not Pompey, Crassus or Caesar saw the point of that argument in the late 50s, these thoughts were no doubt some consolation to Cicero at a time when he was forced to make a number of speeches on behalf of the triumvirs' supporters. These included Vatinius and Gabinius, a supporter of Pompey and former governor of Syria who had had to make way for Crassus. Cicero had first tried, and failed, to prosecute him for *maiestas* (treason), and soon after was forced by Pompey to defend him on a charge of extortion. The case of Rabirius Postumus was connected: he had been accused of receiving some of the money extorted by Gabinius. The speech **Pro M. Aemilio Scauro** was another extortion case (fragments survive in Asconius' commentary; here it is the Sardinian provincials who are characteristically described as unreliable bandits). The speech **Pro Cn. Plancio** was different. Cicero defended him from the charge of having used bribery in an election for the aedileship. Since Plancius as quaestor of Macedonia had helped Cicero during his exile, Cicero can represent the case (in the published version) as yet another attack on himself.

For a time, Cicero thought that he would have to show his support for the dynasts in another way, by acting as legate of Pompey in Sardinia. His brother Quintus had gone to Gaul as one of Caesar's legates; the surviving correspondence between the two brothers has to refer to Caesar in none but the most positive terms. At one point Cicero pretended that he would devote himself to writing an epic celebrating Caesar's British campaign. Another important figure who now joined Caesar as a legate was Mark Antony, who had been active in pacifying Judaea as legate of Gabinius.

But in 53 the political situation was unexpectedly altered by the defeat and death of Crassus, together with his eldest son, by the Parthians at the battle of Carrhae. The three dynasts became two, whose rivalry was sharpened since the death of Pompey's wife Julia in 54 had broken the family connection between them. Pompey strengthened his position further by marrying Cornelia, widow of the younger Crassus: that gave him access both to the support of the Scipios, and more crucially to many of the surviving clients of Crassus.

Fig. 14 Bust of Pompey (Copenhagen).

While Caesar strengthened his hold over Gaul, as well as over an army which observers (including Cicero's correspondents) realised was unmatched in its fighting potential, Pompey looked for ways of tightening his grip over metropolitan politics. He allowed Clodius' supporters to riot unhindered, thus preventing consular elections from being held for the year 52. The security of Rome was not improved when a rival gang was organised by T. Annius Milo, husband of Sulla's daughter Fausta (whose mother was the Metella previously married to Scaurus, thus linking Milo both to the Metelli and to Cicero). For eight months no elections could be held; Pompey bided his time, waiting for the rioting to become so serious that he would be called to restore order by force. The occasion came with the murder of Clodius while on a journey outside Rome on January 18th, 52. Subsequent rioting led to the burning down of the Senate House during Clodius' cremation.

The Senate called on Pompey to be sole consul, *consul sine collega*; Appian rightly refers to monarchical power, 'ἡ μόναρχος ἐξουσία' (Appian, BC 2, 3.20). There was no longer any political pluralism at Rome; with Clodius already out of the way, Pompey now had sole control of Roman politics. In due course he would deal with Caesar; in the meantime he acted to eliminate one of the last independent political figures, Milo. It was in Cicero's interest for there to be a plurality of such figures (in this respect, a live Clodius to attack was preferable to a murdered one). In direct opposition to Pompey, Cicero defended Milo at his trial for Clodius' murder, held on April 4th-8th, 52. On the final day, demonstrations by Clodius' supporters or (according to other sources) the presence of Pompey's soldiers either shattered his nerve, or at any rate persuaded him not to speak clearly. Milo was convicted, and joined Verres in exile at Massilia. After the conviction, Cicero soon recovered his composure, and circulated the **Pro Milone**, a brilliant written version of what, he claimed, he had intended to say, chiefly attacking Clodius as responsible for all Rome's recent civil discord. (When he read the speech, Milo is said to have expressed delight that it was never delivered, since acquittal would have prevented him from ever enjoying the sea-food of Massilia: Dio 40, 53.2f.) Once again, Cicero was prepared to justify violence for political ends:

> If there is any occasion when a man can justifiably be killed –
> and there are many such occasions – then this occasion was
> certainly not only justifiable, but necessary.
>
> (*Pro Milone* 4)

As sole consul, Pompey found it easier to eliminate rivals than to solve the old question of how a monarchical position could be legitimated within the framework of a republican ideology. It is most unlikely that Cicero's references in the *De republica* to a governor (*moderator* or *procurator rei publicae*) who would have general oversight of policymaking in his ideal republic were intended as a justification of Pompey's position: if the *moderator* was more than just any concerned citizen playing his part in public life, then he would have been Cicero himself. It has been suggested that Cicero's ideas about a *moderator* show that he saw the problems caused by the lack of a single political authority at Rome. The control Pompey exercised over Rome looked forward to the emperors' concern for the state as their personal affair.

Like Sulla before him, and Caesar and Augustus later, Pompey justified his control of Rome by claiming that legal reforms were necessary to restore the traditional order. Decrees against corruption included changes to the system of appointing provincial governors, and there is evidence that Pompey planned to preside over the first codification of Roman law in four centuries since the Twelve Tables. Isidore of Seville's summary of the history of Roman law explicitly states that 'Pompey as consul was the first who wanted to have the laws codified in book form, but he gave the idea up for fear of criticism' (*Etymologies* 5, 1.5: 'Leges autem redigere in libris primus consul Pompeius instituere voluit, sed non perseveravit obtrectatorum metu': admittedly a late source). The leading jurist Servius Sulpicius Rufus is said to have provided him with advice on procedure (the anecdote is needlessly associated with Pompey's first consulship). Cicero joined in. Following on from the *De Oratore* and the *De Re Publica*, he composed the **De Legibus** (*On the Laws*), a six-book dialogue containing proposals for a constitution for Rome that would work in practice.

Most of the first three books survive, including Book 1, in which Cicero justifies his ideas partly by emphasising his own authority (his unparalleled expertise in ancient and contemporary history, law, poetry and philosophy as well as rhetoric), but mainly on the grounds that his proposals look to the Natural Law of the Stoics, and are therefore not based on sectional interests. This is one text in which Cicero plays on his links with Marius (see p. 15 above), and he exploits the dialogue form in order to represent himself as arguing in favour of the power of the tribunes on practical grounds, while ascribing the view that they only caused trouble and ought to be abolished to his fellow-speakers Quintus and Atticus (*De Legibus* 3, 19/26).

Chapter 11
Cicero the *Imperator*

The *De Legibus* probably remained unfinished because Cicero found himself obliged to leave Rome for a year to serve as governor of Cilicia. Pompey's decrees against corruption had resulted in an experimental new system of only appointing magistrates to provinces five years after the end of their term of elected office (this was intended to prevent candidates from spending money on largesse in the hope that they would be able to recoup their bribes at the expense of provincials within a couple of years). Consequently it was necessary for ex-magistrates who had not held a provincial command to fill the five-year gap before those who currently held office became available for governorships. Cicero was allocated Cilicia, where his grand-uncle Gratidius had died as a legate of Antonius fifty years earlier, and which had recently been governed by his friend Lentulus Spinther. He left Rome on May 1st, 51; the journey took three months.

The year away from Rome may not have been what Cicero would have chosen, and it had greater political disadvantages for him than it would have had for others. Like any governor, he would of course be cut off from knowing just how Caesar intended to challenge Pompey's control over Rome, and from intervening in that challenge (the surviving book of letters from M. Caelius to Cicero, *Ad Fam.* 8, shows how eager Cicero was for any snippet of information about developments at Rome). But it also prevented him from keeping his image in the forefront of public perception by doing what he was best at, making speeches and later circulating improved versions of them. Caesar was facing a similar problem in Gaul, but had the advantage that he could spend his winters in the Cisalpine part of his province. There he could find Latin books and Latin speakers (like the family of Catullus at Verona) who would pass stories of his intellectual brilliance on to metropolitan Italy (not always unambiguously: cf. Catullus 93). Caesar spent any free moment during his governorship writing – including the works on rhetorical style and on Latin grammar with which he challenged Cicero's intellectual primacy. Cilicia was several months away from Italy, and Cicero only had one winter there. Although he wrote a very large number of letters, it seems a strange failure on his part that he produced no known pamphlets during his governorship. Later, during Caesar's dictatorship, he realised that if he could not publish critical political speeches, he could produce and circulate masses of literary material of a different kind.

Absence from Rome meant absence from domestic as well as public decision-making. While he was away, Terentia arranged a marriage for their daughter Tullia with the Caesarian Publius Cornelius Dolabella. In his letters, Cicero claimed that he had no knowledge of this marriage – though this was a highly convenient claim, since embarrassingly Dolabella was about to prosecute Cicero's predecessor as governor, Appius Claudius.

Nevertheless, it is wrong to see the year as wasted. The exercise of independent military *imperium* gave Cicero the opportunity to claim status in an area in which he had played no part since his youth, but which was becoming more and more crucial – that of military glory.

The military danger to Cilicia was real enough, following Crassus' unprovoked and disastrous attempt to conquer the Parthians from Syria in 53. A Parthian raid on the Syrian capital, Antioch, was foiled by C. Cassius Longinus, acting as quaestorian governor. The Parthians might attack further north, in the Anatolian highlands, as well as in Syria itself. Cicero mustered his troops at Iconium in order to protect the Roman client state of Cappadocia. He also summoned help from another client king, Deiotarus of Galatia, to whom he sent his son and nephew for safe-keeping. When he heard of Cassius' successful defence of Syria, Cicero was able to switch his troops to the Amanus mountains which divided Cilicia from the Orontes valley in Syria. Here Cicero fought two campaigns whose military purpose was to show that Rome was not a broken reed. The first campaign brought him the ceremonial acclamation of *Imperator* by his soldiers. In the autumn, a two months' siege led to the capitulation of a fortress called Pindenissus on December 13th (see p. 62 on the Roman calendar). The Senate voted Cicero a *supplicatio* (festival of thanksgiving), as it had frequently found itself doing for Caesar. We may note that Cicero did not show more Stoic humanity in his treatment of the defeated Cilicians than any other Roman commander would have done. They were killed or enslaved (Cicero refers to the 120,000 sesterces he got from slave-traders after the capture of Pindenissus).

How serious was Cicero in representing himself as a military figure? He was of course playing a political game: to break free of Pompey, and to represent himself as a political figure of the same kind, if not on the same level, as Pompey and Caesar. That would give him a position which both of them would have to take into account in their own rivalry. Again, Cicero exploited his knowledge of Greek history: after his first victory he encamped at Issus, where Alexander the Great had defeated the Persians in 333 BC – not so much in imitation of Alexander as of Pompey, who was constantly pretending to be a Roman Alexander. In his private correspondence, Cicero could make jokes about this, for instance when he writes about having read Xenophon's *Cyropaedia* as a military governor's handbook (a theme which occurs elsewhere in Latin literature), or refers to the imperatorial title as meaningless (*appellatione inani*) in a letter to Atticus, who as an Epicurean pretended to have no concern about military victories (*Ad Att.* 5, 20.4). But other letters show clearly that he hoped he could talk up his successes so much that he would be awarded a triumph by those at Rome who would welcome a third force beside Pompey and Caesar.

Fig. 15 Coin (Cistophorus) struck at Apamea in Phrygia during Cicero's administration of Cilicia. It bears the legend 'CICERO M.F. PROCOS'.

One other aspect of Cicero's governorship may be mentioned. His letters to Rome contain much emphasis on the honesty of his administration, with talk of his own justice, moderation and clemency (*iustitia, abstinentia, clementia*). He made sure that Rome was informed of the contrast between him and his predecessor Appius Claudius Pulcher (cos. 54): he dispensed the provincial cities from sending the expected embassies to Rome praising Pulcher. But the moral high ground was only worth occupying if everyone at Rome knew about it. Hence the very large number of letters which he sent home from Cilicia (2+ books to Atticus alone). In the circumstances it was embarrassing that Marcus Brutus should have written to Cicero asking him to ignore Cicero's own provincial edict by collecting debts resulting from interest charged at 4% per month on loans Brutus had made to the city of Salamis on Cyprus, which was within Cicero's province. Cicero did not dare either to refuse or to oblige Brutus, and left the affair to his successor to sort out.

Cicero left his province on July 30th and was back in Italy on November 24th. He arrived outside Rome with his lictors on January 4th, 49 (the Roman calendar was running two or three months ahead, so this corresponded to autumn 50 in real terms). He stayed outside the sacred boundary of the city (the *pomerium*), thus retaining his promagisterial power to command troops. Ostensibly this was because he hoped that the Senate would award him a triumph for his victory in the Amanus mountains. But he will also have thought of the advantages of holding an independent power of command in the context of the final showdown between Pompey and Caesar.

It was Caesar's intention to win election in 49 to a second consulship without first being destroyed by his enemies through a political trial. It was crucial for Caesar to maintain a high profile through the use of literary propaganda while away from Rome. Apart from works on grammatical and stylistic questions which were intended to show that he rivalled Cicero, and was far superior to Pompey, in these subjects, he produced his *Commentarii* chronicling the conquest of Gaul to ensure that the Roman electorate would support him in 49. Pompey had promised that he could be a candidate in 49 while still governing his province; this would prevent anyone from bringing a prosecution against him. But if the new decree of 52 about provincial governorships superseded that agreement, then Caesar's Gallic command too could be allocated to someone else by the Senate before Caesar could win a second consulship.

That would mean the end of Caesar's political career. After protracted negotiations aiming at a compromise had borne no fruit, Caesar preferred to make use of the superior military force he had at his command, and invaded Italy with his army in the autumn of 50 (early 49 by the contemporary calendar). Pompey thought that if he withdrew to Greece, Caesar would be caught between the Pompeian legions in Spain, and Pompey's client-kings in the East; he could then re-enact Sulla's occupation of Italy thirty years before. But Caesar swiftly destroyed the Spanish army, crossed over to Epirus, and after some serious initial setbacks defeated Pompey and his supporters at Pharsalus in 48; Pompey fled to Egypt, hoping to mobilise the support of Ptolemy Auletes' son, but instead was murdered on landing. In the following years Caesar destroyed his remaining Roman opponents in Africa (with the suicide of Cato at Utica in 46) and in Spain (at the battle of Munda in 45).

Cicero's actions during this period have often been interpreted as the result of vacillation and an inability to decide where his loyalties lay. On the contrary, Cicero was as firmly opposed as ever to allowing an individual politician to break the rules protecting the 'level playing field' of republican politics. But he also knew that, in different circumstances, Pompey had been, and would be again, as ready to ignore the rules as Caesar. Consequently Cicero consistently tried to maintain his own political independence against both Caesar and Pompey. He refused to give legitimacy to Caesar's occupation of Rome in 49, just as he at first refused to join Pompey in Greece, and after Pharsalus he rejected a request to continue the war as head of the Pompeian party (he was almost killed for this refusal by one of Pompey's sons). His independence as a promagistrate with *imperium* by itself created a limited political pluralism in which his personal rhetorical skills, the ability to create a majority through argument rather than force, would continue to be required and acclaimed. Once Caesar had won sole power at Pharsalus, it gradually became clear that this 'republican' view of politics was no longer realistic. Unlike other 'republicans', Cicero saw no point in denying Caesar legitimacy. He returned to Italy with his lictors, still formally a Roman promagistrate. He found himself kept under arrest at Brundisium by Mark Antony, whose step-father Lentulus had been executed on Cicero's orders in 63. Antony pretended to know nothing of any promise by Caesar that Cicero could return to Rome, and Caesar was engaged at Alexandria during the winter of 48/47, installing Cleopatra on her brother's throne. Cicero was not allowed to leave Brundisium until 25th September (= June), 47. When he reached Rome, he finally dismissed his lictors, in accordance with custom.

Chapter 12
Cicero the Writer

Cicero used his enforced leisure from political involvement to produce a flow of writings which ensured that the Roman élite could not forget him. His primary aim was that he would continue to be seen as a potential political actor. Hence he published three speeches delivered in Caesar's presence. These **Caesarian Orations** were not simply panegyrics listing the dictator's virtues. The **Pro Marcello** had not been solicited by Caesar. In it Cicero gives him specific political advice. If Caesar wanted to retain supreme power, he would have to legitimate it not just by claiming that he was bringing about a return to proper order (e.g. through his reform of the calendar), but by addressing the social and moral issues which contemporaries felt had led to a preference for violence over legality and compromise through debate. He would also have to exercise the Stoic virtue of self-control in restraint of his monarchical power. These points also occur in the **Pro Ligario**, defending a Pompeian supporter from a charge of treason.

If Cicero addressed Caesar in these speeches with language appropriate to a monarch, then that reflected the reality of Caesar's exercise of power. In particular, the **Pro Rege Deiotaro**, in which Cicero defended his friend the Galatian king against the accusation of having tried to kill Caesar, looks forward to the way in which the emperors later took decisions not in any public forum, but through their household *consilium*. Caesar acted as though he alone was responsible for policy-making at Rome, and not surprisingly he failed to reconcile the traditional political élite to his way of doing things. But we should be cautious about assuming that he wanted to be seen formally as a monarch, still less as a Hellenistic king. During his ten years away in Gaul, Caesar had not had to act as though he was only one leader amongst several in the Senate, and his behaviour during the short periods when he was present at Rome during the civil war period shows that he was impatient with senatorial procedure and the time-consuming consultations of an open political system. (On one occasion, Cicero tells us that he had found his own name included amongst the proposers of a particular motion, although Caesar had not bothered to consult him.) So it was not surprising that those who wished to denigrate him could represent Caesar as wanting to be a king. They included some who wanted a return to republican pluralism and open politics, but also anyone who might wish to replace Caesar at the pinnacle of power: specifically Mark Antony, who had been rumoured to have planned to have Caesar assassinated during the siege of Massilia in 49. It was Antony who, much to Caesar's annoyance, hailed Caesar as 'king' in a famous incident during the festival of the Lupercalia in February 44; his intention is likely to have been to embarrass Caesar, not to praise him. Caesar swiftly proclaimed that Jupiter was the only king of the Romans, but the damage had been done.

Fig. 16 Denarius depicting Caesar as *Pontifex Maximus*, wearing a golden wreath associated with the Etruscan kings. Caesar's use of symbols that could be interpreted as monarchical played into the hands of those who wished to kill him.

The centralisation of power in the dictator's hands was only one reason why the political élite resented him. Paradoxically, Caesar's attempt, through his much-trumpeted *clementia*, to reconcile those sections of the élite which had supported Pompey caused even more resentment. Civil wars, by eliminating those on the losing side from public life, frequently have the function of opening up new opportunities to those who have supported the winner. But in addition to promising magistracies and senatorial rank to his own supporters, Caesar made a point of trying to win the support of his erstwhile opponents by appointing them to offices as well. The traditional number of magistracies did not suffice to satisfy both groups. So in order to fulfil his commitments, Caesar had to increase both the number of senators (to over a thousand, according to some sources) and the number of those given magisterial office – in 45, as many as forty praetors were appointed. This devalued the status of the honours Caesar bestowed, and alienated both groups – his own supporters and the ex-Pompeians he was trying to reconcile. The clearest example was the appointment of Caninius Rebilus to a suffect consulship on December 31st, 45, when the ordinary consul, the patrician Quintus Fabius Maximus, died on the day before his term came to an end. Previous holders of the consular office naturally felt that Caesar was insulting the republic by demeaning its magistracies.

The slogan *concordia* had frequently played an important role in Cicero's own attempts to mobilise majorities in his speeches; so it is not surprising that he should have accommodated himself to Caesar's policy of *clementia* publicly in speeches like the *Pro Marcello*, and privately by corresponding both with Caesar's supporters and with republicans, including some still in exile. Whether he took *concordia* seriously as a solution to the political rivalries which it in fact exacerbated by increasing the number of those chasing public office, is another question. He even entertained Caesar himself to dinner at his villa at Cumae, on December 19th, 45 (he was not so happy about entertaining the 2,000 soldiers Caesar brought along as his bodyguard). For such a meeting to work at all, the conversation had to be entirely about literature; on that level the rivalry between the two greatest exponents of Latin oratory (and we may recall how Caesar artifically set himself up as the exponent of an Attic purity in Latin in contrast to the 'Asianism' of Cicero) could be resolved.

> Nevertheless my guest was not the kind whom one would invite
> to come again soon. Once was enough.
>
> (*Ad Att.* 13, 52)

After his release from confinement at Brundisium, Cicero switched his energies towards philosophical writing. This has traditionally been seen as an admission that the political sphere had to be abandoned to Caesar and his supporters, a sign of despair about politics and a compensatory turning to something which was a substitute. But as well as accepting Caesar's political supremacy, Cicero was choosing other means to rival him, by asserting his own superiority as an orator and as an expert on Greek philosophy. That unparalleled access to Greek philosophy in turn allowed Cicero to challenge Caesar's primacy in another way, by laying claim to the high ground of morality.

Two pamphlets on rhetoric came first in 46, the **Brutus** and the **Orator**. Both discussed the relative merits of the contrasting rhetorical styles labelled 'Asianism' and 'Atticism'. Cicero ridiculed the extreme Atticist position, pointing out for instance that it was absurd to take the speeches of Thucydides' history as paradigms for a speech addressed to any real audience – no one would understand them. A good orator would know how to use all three styles – grand, medium, and plain – in the appropriate context: and he refers to some of his own speeches to show that that was what he himself had done. The implication was that he, not Caesar, deserved to be recognised as the best kind of public speaker.

Only then did Cicero begin to write a cycle of philosophical texts. His first concern was to deal with ethics, or practical morality (one important issue discussed in the *De Natura Deorum* is the relationship between divine providence and individual ethical responsibility). Whether he planned to complete the encyclopaedia by writing about physics or natural history ('natural philosophy') is disputed. Although fragments survive from a translation of Plato's *Timaeus*, it is not clear whether these were intended to fit into some broader work on physics, and in any case it is clear that he left that topic until last. What concerned him was to provide an ethical code which would describe in language which ordinary Italians could understand the kind of public and private morality which he saw himself as having upheld over the years. In some texts written after Caesar's death, criticism of Caesar's moral stand is made explicit; and even in 45 Cicero describes the unhappiness of a tyrant (*Tusculans* 5, 20.56ff.). The implication is perhaps that in spite of appearances, he has been a more successful and happier man than Caesar.

More personal motives, much emphasised by past scholarship on Cicero, may have played a role too. It is not helpful to speculate on whether Cicero turned to philosophy to escape the unhappiness of his marriage (of over 30 years' standing) to Terentia, which had broken down during Cicero's absence in Greece and Brindisi, and of his subsequent divorce. (He later married a teenage girl called Publilia.) A more persuasive case can be made out for the effect of the death of Cicero's daughter Tullia in February 45. This turned Cicero's thoughts to questions of mortality and immortality, as can be seen from his correspondence; but we should not construct an opposition between his private/philosophical and his public/political life. Another personal factor may have been just as important in making Cicero turn to writing about personal morality, duties and loyalty, namely disappointment at his brother Quintus Cicero's support for Caesar, and shock at finding that Quintus' son was trying to win preferment from Caesar by blaming Cicero, his uncle, for their own earlier support of Pompey. In 45, the young Quintus joined Caesar's campaign against the Pompeians in Spain, and Cicero's son Marcus would have liked to go as well. Whether Cicero thought that this would be too public a betrayal of earlier loyalties, or rather was concerned that Caesar might not win the Spanish campaign, and that Marcus might not survive it, he used his paternal authority to send his son out of the way of political involvement, to Athens. The overt reason was that young Marcus was to study rhetoric and philosophy there.

The search for constancy, for a moral fixed point, at a time of shifting personal and political loyalties, was expressed in two essays now lost, a **Consolatio** on the death of Tullia, in which Cicero comforted himself with arguments about the comparative insignificance of mortal life taken from Hellenistic consolation literature, and the famous dialogue **Hortensius**, which St Augustine found so powerful four centuries later that it stimulated him to study philosophy. The dialogue explored ideas about the ultimate purpose and significance of human life, and the meaning of 'eternity'. Cicero's consoling conclusion was that for a wise man, happiness comes from the process of searching for the truth, not from the impossible achievement of actually finding it.

Cicero produced several different versions of the **Academics**. Book 2 of the first version (known as **Lucullus**) survives; the third version was completed in June 45 (*Ad Fam.* 9.8.2). The interlocutors are Atticus and Varro (that Varro and Atticus were close friends may be deduced from the fact that Varro included Atticus as a character in his book on stock-raising, *De Re Rustica* 2). Varro is represented as sceptical about Cicero's entire project to provide an Italian readership with a summary of Greek philosophy: he says that the Greek originals are available to those who are really interested, and that the Latin language lacked the necessary technical vocabulary for philosophical debate. These arguments are reminiscent of Caesar's concern for pure Latinity. (Varro's own interest in 'correct Latin' is revealed in his grammatical works.)

In the five books **De Finibus** (*On the Ends of Good and Evil*), Cicero applies the sceptical approach of the New Academy. In Book 1 L. Manlius Torquatus expounds Epicureanism, to be refuted by Cicero himself in Book 2; in Books 3 and 4, Cato expounds and Cicero criticises the Stoic position; in Book 5, Piso discusses the disagreement between the 'Old' Academy and the Peripatetics as to whether virtue is the sole or the greatest good, a topic Cicero had already adumbrated in the *De*

Legibus. Piso ends by arguing that for practical purposes Antiochus of Ascalon (who tried to turn the Academy away from Scepticism and back to what he thought had been Plato's position) and the Stoics teach the same thing.

The **Tusculan Disputations** are in the form of declamatory exercises between master and disciple on the importance of real virtue: they take place on the five days between 16th and 20th June 46. The theme of Book 1 is death; Book 2, pain; Book 3, suffering; Book 4, overcoming the passions; and Book 5 on the sufficiency of virtue for happiness. The *Tusculans* are dedicated to Brutus, whose family laid claim to descent from the man who had expelled the kings from Rome. This makes it appropriate for Cicero to include a critique of the unhappiness of a tyrant (*Tusculans* 5, 20.56ff.) – the tyrant being the Greek Dionysius of Syracuse. Laelius and his one consulship are compared favourably with Cinna's four: in 46 BC, Caesar was elected consul for a fourth time for 45, without a colleague. Hence the dialogue will have been seen to carry a contemporary resonance.

Another treatise dedicated to Brutus was the **De Natura Deorum** (*On the Nature of the Gods*, late 45). It recounts a fictional discussion on the gods and their care for humanity, located in 77/75 BC. In Book 1 the Epicurean Velleius, and in Book 2 the Stoic Balbus, expound the different views of their respective schools, to be subjected to a critique by Cotta as a follower of Scepticism. During the Middle Ages, the *De Natura Deorum* was an important source for Christian arguments in support of monotheism, and in the Enlightenment it was equally important as a source for arguments against inherited religious beliefs. Given the amount of writing Cicero was producing during this period, it is hardly surprising that some of it was recycled. Several pages in the *De Natura Deorum* are taken from his early translation of Aratus' *Phaenomena* (see p. 21 above). Most of the material is from Greek sources, but there are occasional passages relevant to Rome – for instance, Cotta attacks the cult of Romulus (3, 16/40), a clear warning to anyone who thought that Caesar could be turned into a god. The ending is curious: it leaves the reader with the impression that Cicero himself is inclined towards Stoic belief in God, but too much of a Sceptic to commit himself.

The essay **De Senectute** (*On Old Age*) covers a series of points, some dealing with Cicero's personal anxieties at this time, others reclaiming a public role. Cicero was now 62. At the age of 65, Romans were no longer expected to play an active part in public life. To make clear his availability for further service to the state should it be required, Cicero points out that the great political figures of the past continued to give advice, if not to lead armies, in their old age. He particularly emphasises Fabius Maximus, the general in the Second Punic War who wore down Hannibal, since Fabius too suffered the premature death of a child; and so did Cato the Elder, the speaker in the dialogue, with whom Cicero had already identified as a 'new man' like himself. Mention of agriculture as something to do in retirement at Tusculum gives Cicero an excuse to include material from his early translation of Xenophon's *Oeconomicus*.

The **De Divinatione** was sent to Atticus before April 7th, 44, soon after Caesar's murder. Like the **De Fato**, it is based on Posidonius' Stoic discussions about the relationship between the natural and the divine world. The crucial point Cicero makes is the insistence that divine providence does not take away personal responsibility, in particular at the level of community affairs.

Chapter 13

Caesar and his Political Successors

Caesar's supremacy could not be challenged while he was away from Rome except by superior military force. But during the short periods of time he spent in the city, it was different: there he had to act either with or without the political class, and either way that class found his actions offensive. After the battle of Munda, Caesar spent the winter of 45/44 in Rome, and he soon came to realise that the only way to head off opposition to his style of government was by going away again. If he were to do that, he would have to find another war to fight. A cause was to hand: to avenge Crassus' defeat at the hands of the Parthians nine years before. That winter, Caesar prepared for a major expedition; the date set for his departure from Rome was March 18th. He appointed magistrates to hold office at Rome in his absence for the next three years. The story goes that during this time, after conquering Parthia, he intended to continue with India and China before returning via southern Russia. Some twenty legions were sent East, the greatest concentration of Roman legions there had ever been. Caesar also sent his grand-nephew, Gaius Octavius (as he then was), East, initially to Apollonia in Epirus in order to immerse himself in Greek culture. That gives us an important indication as to Caesar's aim: it was not just to escape from criticism at Rome, nor was it just to win more military glory for himself – his earlier campaigns had brought him sufficient glory; it was to ensure the succession of Octavius by taking him with him on the campaign. If Octavius shared the military prestige accruing from the greatest war the Romans had ever fought, then in three years' time at the age of 22 he would be in an unchallengeable political position: the concentration of power would have become hereditary.

That threat mobilised a coalition of earlier supporters of Caesar who felt that he had not sufficiently rewarded them, and of others who felt stifled by his supremacy and calculated that they would do better in the competitive pluralism of a republic. The original leader of the conspiracy was Gaius Cassius: since Crassus' defeat in 53, he had been Rome's leading expert in military relations with Parthia. Praetor in 44, he would have been a natural choice as a legate in any major operation against Parthia; but Caesar had passed him over. Others who had supported Caesar but were dissatisfied with the promotion being held out to them were Gaius Trebonius (who had been suffect consul in 45, and a close associate of Caesar's for over ten years) and Decimus Brutus (another of Caesar's legates in Gaul), who had been promised a consulship in 42 but who may have felt he had as good a claim to an independent political power-base as others: in particular, Caesar's lieutenant and rival, Antony.

Caesar's appointment of people many of whom thought they deserved high office even without his patronage, not only failed to reconcile these appointees but also had the effect of blocking promotion for others who felt that they were more deserving, or would have had a better chance of winning office under a system of open, competitive elections. That was the system for which 'genuine republicans' yearned: a system in which inherited influence, and the wealth required to win the favour of the electorate, played a more prominent role than administrative capability or loyalty to the dynast. Marcus Brutus, whose family background (leaving aside personal ability) guaranteed him a good chance of success under such a system, was invited to head the conspiracy at a later stage: as a descendant of the hero who had rid Rome of the Tarquins, his name alone was an ideal rallying point for those who represented Caesar as a king from whom Rome needed to be liberated.

Cicero was not invited to join them. There was no need: his writings constantly made it clear that he saw Caesar as a rival in more than just literary terms, and he could be expected to welcome the return of a system in which the process of decision-making required persuasion to produce majorities out of the different factions. There may also have been a more direct motive. Cicero's authority and his political ambition were such that he might become more than just a symbol of republicanism. Cassius and Brutus did not want to throw off Caesar's supremacy to replace it by Cicero's, no matter how much they may have respected him. Less flatteringly, they may not have trusted him to keep their plans secret. It was far better to leave him uninvolved, so that he would support their actions as, notionally, an independent figure – as he indeed did when the conspirators struck on March 15th, three days before Caesar was due to have left Rome and put himself beyond their reach.

The extent to which the Roman political élite seemed happy that the removal of Caesar would allow them to pursue their competition for honours without interference or guidance is revealed by the fact that Caesar's colleague as consul, Mark Antony, was prepared to accept a compromise put forward at a meeting of the Senate on March 17th by which the assassins were granted immunity, while Caesar's official actions (*acta*) were confirmed. Cicero played a major role in this debate, parading his knowledge of Greek history by citing as a precedent the amnesty given to the 'Thirty Tyrants' after the democratic victory at Athens in 403 BC. For the first time, those in the Senate who wanted a return to political pluralism were prepared to listen to his pleas for compromise with respect and attention.

What they failed to take account of was the loyalty of both the urban plebs of Rome and the army to Caesar, who had consistently acted as the patron and protector of both groups. When after a couple of days Antony realised the force of this loyalty, he sought to mobilise it in his own interest. Having persuaded the Senate on March 18th that reconciliation required a state funeral for Caesar, he used the occasion to foment a serious riot which enabled him to take control of the city, and force Cassius, Brutus, and Cicero himself to leave. Cicero's correspondence during the next few months shows that he saw Antony as having stepped into Caesar's position, and it bitterly criticises the conspirators for having failed to deal with him too on the Ides of March.

But by having assumed Caesar's position so rapidly, Antony had also inherited the resentment of the political class – whether they had earlier supported Pompey or Caesar – against Caesar's monopolisation of power. Men who had been supporters of Caesar preferred to compete openly against each other rather than depend for future promotion on Antony as they had had to depend on Caesar. One such figure was Dolabella, whom Caesar had appointed to look after Rome during the Parthian campaign. He had no intention of acting as Antony's lieutenant in the same way. If Antony controlled Rome, then it was to the Senate that Dolabella had to look for support; and the Senate duly appointed him to the consulship left vacant by Caesar's death. Dolabella had been Cicero's son-in-law for a time; Cicero wrote to him (*Ad Fam.* 9.14 = *Ad Att.* 14, 17A) trying to pin him down to an alliance against Antony, but Dolabella's interest in pluralism extended only to enabling himself to negotiate with Antony from a position of strength. Dolabella knew that under the present circumstances only military force could guarantee such strength, and had himself appointed to a five-year term as governor of Syria, where Caesar had concentrated his army for the abortive Parthian war.

In the event, a much more significant actor had returned to Italy to challenge Antony's pre-eminence, namely Caesar's grand-nephew Octavius, with whom he had intended to share the glory of the conquest of Parthia, and whom he had instituted as his principal heir in his will.

In accordance with Roman practice, Octavius assumed Caesar's name to show that he had stepped into his legal persona (though we may note that whatever Caesar's long-term intentions may have been, Octavius had not been adopted as his son during Caesar's lifetime – there was no such thing as adoption by will under Roman law). But 'Caesar Octavianus' (as he was entitled to call himself) was as unwilling as Dolabella or any other Caesarian to accept Antony's hegemony, and like Dolabella, he turned to the Senate to seek legitimation for his position. He had the very great advantage of being so young (he would only be nineteen on September 23rd, 44) that few people, at that point, imagined that he would soon be at the centre of the political stage (even Pompey had been four years older when he raised an army in support of Sulla in 83).

Cicero's correspondence shows his awareness of the danger if Octavius (Octavian) were to be allowed any independent political authority. In May, he reprimanded Gaius Matius for arranging games at Rome in Caesar's honour and on Octavian's behalf. In a letter to Atticus in June, he recognised that Octavian was potentially both an ally of the republican cause against Antony, and a danger:

> In Octavian there is a great deal of talent and natural force, and he seems as positively disposed towards our [sc. republican] heroes as we would like him to be. But we must be seriously concerned about the danger arising from his youth, his position as [Caesar's] heir, and his advisors [especially the Caesarians Oppius and Balbus]. We must pay him very close attention, and do everything to separate him off from Antony.
>
> *(Ad Att.* 15, 12.2)

Like Brutus, Cassius and Dolabella, all of whom were courting the eastern legions, Cicero too knew that control of the East was going to be crucial if force were to be required to challenge Antony's claim to political pre-eminence. Cicero exploited his concern for his son's studies at Athens: he pretended to be so worried about Marcus' progress that he had to go there himself, and asked both Antony and Dolabella, as consuls, to grant him a *libera legatio* (the right to travel in the provinces with the privileges of a Roman legate). Dolabella thought it expedient to appoint him as a legate of his own. If Cicero really was worried about Marcus' progress with his studies, then such worries were self-induced, as is made clear by the report sent home by Gaius Trebonius, who passed through Athens on his way to take up the governorship of Asia (*Ad Fam.* 12.16.1f.).

But that was a course which in the end Cicero failed to take, although he left his villa at Tusculum on July 1st, 44 for southern Italy in order to find a suitable port not controlled by Antony's forces from which to cross the Adriatic. Did he actually want to go East at all? That would have left him in danger of being cut off by Antony's military control of the straits. What Cicero wanted was to be somewhere whence he could return to Rome as quickly as possible if the political opportunity arose. Sicily was more suitable, and better supplied with clients who might recall how Cicero had acted for them a quarter of a century earlier.

On his way south to Rhegium in July 44, Cicero compiled the **Topica**, a short systematic guide to the standard arguments (*topoi*) which orators can use in any particular context, for the benefit of Gaius Trebatius, whose expertise was primarily legal. Trebatius was one of several protégés Cicero might have need of in the coming political showdown with Antony, and Cicero wanted to develop Trebatius' oratorical skills. He also wrote an essay *De Gloria*, in great haste and without proper library facilities. He subsequently discovered that he had already used the same preface for Book 3 of the *Academics*.

Chapter 14
Philippics

Cicero did in fact arrive at Syracuse on August 1st, 44, but instead of sailing East – if that had indeed been his intention – he returned to Rome. The reason was that he heard that, on the same day, Antony's claim to political supremacy had been publicly challenged in the Senate by a senior consular, Piso, the Caesarian who had failed to protect Cicero from Clodius in 58. Cicero knew that the moment had come to speak out, in support for, or out of rivalry with, Piso. He arrived back in Rome on August 31st: Antony had summoned a meeting of the Senate for the following day, in order to re-assert his authority. Troops were deployed to cow the opposition. Antony persuaded the Senate to vote Caesar divine honours, thus representing himself (rather than Octavian) as Caesar's political successor. Cicero diplomatically claimed that he was too exhausted from his journey to be able to attend.

But Antony was not able to be present at another meeting of the Senate on the following day, September 2nd. It was chaired by Dolabella, who allowed Cicero to speak, not because he had once been his father-in-law, but because it would have been agreeable to see Antony needled again in public. Cicero's speech was later published as the **First Philippic**, the first of the cycle of fourteen speeches in which Cicero represented his opposition to Antony as analogous to Demosthenes' mobilisation of Athenian resistance to Philip of Macedon in the fourth-century BC. In it he explains why he had left Rome over the summer and why he had decided to return now rather than wait until the new consuls Hirtius and Pansa had taken up office on January 1st (although both were ex-Caesarians, that did not make them supporters of Antony). He went on, without mentioning Antony by name, to attack the Caesarian stance he had taken since Caesar's death, beginning with the divine honours for Caesar decreed the previous day. In particular, Cicero gave expression to latent disapproval of the way in which Antony had assumed Caesar's monopoly of power by criticising his misuse of the *acta Caesaris*. These *acta* were decisions taken by Caesar (and covered by the Senate's ratification of his *acta*) but not published. They were therefore open to interpretation or invention by Antony, who was in physical possession of Caesar's notebooks.

Fig. 17 Antony.

Antony clearly understood the importance of Cicero's attack. On September 19th, he countered with a carefully prepared speech in which he tried to isolate Cicero by representing him as systematically responsible for the collapse of political order: he cited the execution of Catiline's supporters, the murder of Clodius, the breakdown of friendship between Caesar and Pompey, and Caesar's assassination. Cicero's reply took the form of the **Second Philippic**. It is a striking example of literary invective; but its political and primary purpose was to counter Antony's attempt to isolate Cicero from 'ordinary, decent, peace-loving Senators' by identifying Antony in his turn as typical of everything that they disapproved of, as totally devoid of the Roman virtues of courage, self-control, financial and sexual integrity and so on.

Although written in the form of a speech to the Senate, it is far longer than a speech could have been. Cicero had it circulated as part of a semi-secret campaign to create a position of strength for himself under the new consuls of 43, Hirtius and Pansa. Hirtius had been one of the

Caesarian protégés, like Trebatius, with whom Cicero had been practising declamation, in order to groom him for a political role in the pluralist Senate Cicero was hoping to re-establish. The enormous number of letters Cicero wrote during that autumn was part of the same campaign. This was 'networking' on a grand scale: Cicero wanted to ensure that his existence, and his plans for a political order without Antony, would be foremost in the consciousness of those with access to potential military force, including Cassius and Brutus, Trebonius in Asia, Quintus Cornificius in Africa, Decimus Brutus in Cisalpine Gaul, and Munatius Plancus in Gallia Comata. Many of these governors had been appointed by Caesar, but as Cicero knew, that did not mean they would necessarily follow Antony, if the pluralist alternative were presented to them as more attractive. What Cicero should not be seen as doing was creating a republican 'party' in any organisational sense. The pluralist politics in which his power of persuasion would have a recognised role consisted of individual political figures, combining on particular issues when persuaded that that would be in their interest. Cicero wanted to make sure that as wide a range of political personalities as possible were persuaded that Antony's removal was indeed in their interest.

Cicero's literary production continued unabated through the autumn of 44. In the **Laelius De Amicitia**, he discussed the moral issues raised by friendship, as practised by the Romans and the Greeks. Cicero took up a position which once again allowed him to claim the moral high ground. The essay was written with as much haste as others that year; one obvious insertion in the argument shows that Cicero was particularly concerned to confront his readership with the question of friendship versus loyalty to the state (§§ 26-43). This was obviously relevant to the men who had just been Caesar's friends and killers, but it was also intended to prepare readers for the coming struggle against Antony. The dialogue's dramatic date is just after Scipio Aemilianus' death in 129 BC; some thought that he had been murdered, like Caesar.

Political motives, too, should perhaps not be excluded from the complex reasons behind the writing of **Duties** (*De Officiis*, long known in English as 'Tully's Offices') in October/November, in which Cicero reminded his readers of his resistance to Chrysogonus early on in his career – resistance which he now represented as opposition to the tyranny of Sulla. The three books of *Duties* have a different format from Cicero's other philosophical works. They represent the characteristically Roman tradition of teaching passed on by a father to his son (in this case Marcus, still away at Athens). Books 1 and 2 discuss the concepts of what is morally decent (*honestum*) and what is advantageous (*utile*), and the third book suggests that there need be no conflict between the two. The main source of books 1 and 2 was the second-century BC Stoic philosopher Panaetius, with Ciceronian additions, e.g. on the superiority of public life over private contemplation (allowing the inference that the reader should not stand aside from a future attempt to oust Antony) and of the contribution of the statesman, the *orator* (i.e. Cicero himself) over that of the military commander. Cicero will have had Antony in mind, though he explicitly attacks Caesar for his deluded search for personal glory at the expense of legality (*De Officiis* 1.26; cf. 64).

At the beginning of October, Antony and Octavian had both left Rome. Decimus Brutus refused to hand over the army in Cisalpine Gaul to Antony: meanwhile Octavian tried to solicit Cicero to his cause, inviting him to join in raising Caesarian troops against Antony in Campania. Cicero's letters to Brutus show that he saw the danger clearly – Octavian for all his youth was potentially a dynast like Antony, and would have to be even more loyal to Caesar's principles (indeed, Octavian had sworn an oath to be so in a *contio* held at Rome in early November). But if Octavian was going to challenge Antony for the role of Caesar's successor, then Brutus, and Cicero himself, might exploit that opportunity to restore pluralism. Antony returned to Rome in late November, probably with the intention of destroying Octavian; in the event he had to leave, since Octavian had persuaded two of the legions which Antony had brought back to Italy from Macedonia in order to fight Decimus Brutus to switch their loyalty to him. At almost the same time (November 28th) Cicero decided to return to Rome, claiming that he had pressing financial problems to deal with (*Ad Att.* 16, 15.6).

He took the opportunity, in the **Third** and **Fourth Philippic** (spoken before the Senate and people respectively) to call for an alliance between the Senate, Octavian, and Decimus Brutus against Antony. He assumed that when the new consuls took office on January 1st, he would be invited to lead the debate in his capacity as senior consular, and mobilise that alliance. But C. Vibius Pansa preferred to call on Fufius Calenus, an old supporter of Clodius, Caesar, and later Antony, who proposed sending a delegation to Antony to work out a compromise. In the **Fifth Philippic**, Cicero unsuccessfully called for the Senate to pass its 'Last Decree' (the SCU) against Antony – which would incidentally have provided further retrospective legitimation of his own actions in 63. More constructively, he hoped to draw M. Aemilius Lepidus, the commander of the Caesarian forces in Nearer Spain, away from Antony with a decree that he be honoured with a gilt equestrian statue.

But the Senate had decided to send the delegation proposed by

Calenus; at a *contio*, Cicero denounced this as a waste of time in the **Sixth Philippic**. In mid-January, he again told the Senate in the **Seventh Philippic** that compromise with Antony was impossible, and indeed Calenus' delegation returned to Rome on February 1st without having obtained anything from Antony. In the **Eighth Philippic**, Cicero attacked Pansa and Calenus for their mistake, and suggested setting a deadline of March 14th: if no satisfaction had been obtained from Antony by then, he should be declared a public enemy. In the **Ninth Philippic**, Cicero explains his reasons for proposing that his old friend the jurist Servius Sulpicius Rufus, who had died in the course of the *legatio* to Antony, should be honoured with a statue, a privilege traditionally only awarded to those who had died of wounds received from the enemy while on such an embassy.

Fig. 18 Gold Aureus struck in Greece for Brutus' war-chest.

In the East meanwhile, Brutus, formally governor of Crete and Cyrene, had prevented Antony's brother Gaius from taking over the legions in Macedonia. Brutus was supported by the previous governor, Q. Hortensius (son of the orator). When Calenus proposed that Brutus be required to relinquish his command, Cicero attacked him bitterly in the **Tenth Philippic**: he succeeded in his purpose, and the Senate gave its support to Brutus. Further east, Dolabella, finding that Cassius was illegally in control of Syria (with its legions), decided to take over the province of Asia instead; this resulted in the death of the legitimate governor Trebonius, who would have been more reliable as an opponent of Antony. Cicero took advantage of a suggestion that one of the consuls should crush Dolabella to make the constitutionally astonishing proposal in the **Eleventh Philippic** that Cassius should be appointed to do so. That would have legitimated Cassius' control of Syria, where most of the army collected for the war against Parthia was still concentrated. On this occasion Cicero failed to carry the day, though he went on to advocate support for Cassius at a *contio*, and wrote to Cassius himself urging him to act without awaiting senatorial approval (*Ad Fam.* 12, 7).

Those in the Senate who wished to avoid the necessity of taking sides against Antony were encouraged by Cicero's failure to have Cassius appointed to govern Syria. They suggested a further senatorial delegation to Antony to seek a compromise. One of the five persons proposed, Servilius Vatia Isauricus, said that he was not prepared to serve, and this enabled Cicero to explain his own reasons for opposing further delay in the **Twelfth Philippic.** The mission was abandoned, and no alternative was left but civil war. Antony circulated a letter in which he argued that there were two irreconcilable parties (*partes*) at Rome; he denigrated those opposed to him as 'Pompeians'. Consequently all who were loyal to Caesar's memory – and he was well aware that the most powerful figures apart from Cicero were in this category – should join him, and not the troublemaking gladiatorial trainer (*lanista*) Cicero.

On March 20th, after Pansa had left Rome to join his colleague Hirtius, the Senate debated letters from Lepidus and L. Munatius Plancus (governing Spain and Gaul), which expressed opposition to military action against Antony. In the **Thirteenth Philippic**, Cicero attacked their view of the situation (the proposal for an equestrian statue of Lepidus now forgotten), and also made a detailed attack on Antony's dishonest attempt to tar his opponents with the 'Pompeian' brush.

The last work Cicero was to circulate, the **Fourteenth Philippic**, was delivered on April 21st: in it Cicero proposed a senatorial thanksgiving for a victory over Antony which the consul Hirtius had won a week before. On the same day, near Mutina, the last army to take its orders from the Senate again defeated Antony; on the 26th, the Senate at last declared him an enemy. But Hirtius fell in the battle, and Pansa died of wounds soon after. Decisions were now taken by those who had actual control over the armies, and it no longer mattered whether majorities could be put together in the Senate. Cicero published no more speeches.

Chapter 15
Failure and Success

The following months saw shifting alliances as Octavian, Plancus and Lepidus calculated whether their advantage lay in the pluralism of a Senatorial republic in which decisions were taken as a result of debate, or in an alliance with Antony or another of the military strongmen. The key figure was Octavian, who was aware that he had more to gain from legitimation by the Senate than by becoming Antony's junior colleague. He invited the Senate to let him stand for the consulship. Such permission would have made it clear that Octavian stood as much above the law as Antony. Cicero knew that he could not afford to let this demand be granted: yet by refusing it, the Senate effectively lost the support of Octavian and his army. In June and July, Cicero wrote several letters to Brutus, appealing to him to ship the Macedonian legions to Italy. But in Brutus' eyes, Cicero had compromised himself too much with the Caesarians. Instead of providing the Senate with an army which might have challenged both Octavian and Antony in Italy, Brutus remained in Macedonia, and was defeated at Philippi in the following year. When Octavian marched on Rome on August 19th and had himself and his cousin Q. Pedius elected consuls, Cicero and the Senate had no armed forces which could prevent them. Octavian now no longer needed their support. Pedius forced the Senate to rescind its enactments against Antony and Lepidus, and in November Octavian, the legitimate consul, agreed to share power with Antony and Lepidus as formal 'Commissioners for the restoration of the republic', *Tresviri reipublicae constituendae causa*. To raise money, they proposed to execute some thousands of wealthy Italians and sequestrate their property. Antony insisted that Cicero, responsible for the death of his step-father Lentulus Sura twenty years before, should be included. He was killed near his villa at Formiae on December 7th, 43.

An account of events in a pluralist political system which is constructed around a single individual has certain obvious limitations. It need only look at the way in which that one individual responded to challenges from his competitors, and not to try to understand the intentions and motivations of a plethora of other, sometimes relatively minor, but independent, actors.

The biographical approach also invites judgement of how that individual affected the course of events. That Cicero was a key figure of his time goes without saying. We have seen that although he had no consular ancestors, his family's relationships through marriage and friendship gave him access to the political centre, where his personal abilities, even though these were intellectual rather than military, brought him election to the highest magistracy. That might already have been achieved by his paternal grandfather, had he wished it, and grand-uncle, had he not died as Antonius' prefect in Cilicia. But it was Cicero's willingness to assimilate every aspect of Greek culture, literary, philo-sophical and rhetorical, that justified his claim that the republic needed him. No one could equal his ability to use persuasive arguments in order to create majorities amongst juries, senators, or citizens at assemblies. That claim also implicitly denied equal importance to other ways of winning fame: through warfare, or violence against the authorities (as practised by *popularis* leaders from the Gracchi on, or Sulla, or Caesar); through successful generalship, as in the case of Pompey; and even through knowledge of Roman law, as with Servius Sulpicius Rufus.

But Cicero's emphasis on persuasion was only valid in a system in which decision-making was open, and where those who decided were presented with alternative courses of action by their leaders. In 44-43, Cicero fought for the survival of the republic partly because it had for centuries proved to be a mechanism for directing the ambitions of powerful individuals for the collective good, but also because only a pluralist system required and rewarded his own ability to persuade through argument. The persuasion exercised by the triumvirs, and the emperors after them, was of a different kind. In the generation after Cicero it was not to rhetoric, but to the security provided by a clear and authoritative system of law that Romans began to look to find certainty and security, no matter how capricious their current ruler might be.

But if the primacy of rhetoric was shortlived, the contribution which Cicero made to Latin culture through his published speeches, and through the philosophical writings which were intended at least to some extent to highlight his status, was a permanent one. Although Cicero's rhetorical style was by no means always accepted as an ideal, its presence in the school syllabus meant that again and again over the centuries it inspired writers to imitate it – beginning with third- and fourth-century Christians like Minucius Felix, Lactantius, Ambrose and Jerome. Later ages were inspired by different works of Cicero's. In the fourteenth century, Coluccio Salutati composed the letters he wrote as secretary to the Florentine government on the lines of Cicero's letters; from the fifteenth century until the nineteenth, Cicero's philosophical works were read as the main source of information about the Hellenistic schools of philosophy. And 'Tully's Offices' was a handbook of good behaviour for Christian gentlemen for centuries.

Did Cicero achieve more than his contemporaries? Crassus, Pompey, Cato, Caelius, Caesar, Brutus, Cassius, Antony – all died violent deaths, and none lived to a greater age than Cicero. (Lucullus apparently died in his bed, but suffering from a debilitating disease, perhaps Alzheimer's, which made him entirely dependent on his doctors and the slaves who fed him.) We are less impressed by Cicero's military achievement in Cilicia than his contemporaries were; and we are, or ought to be, shocked by the way he was sometimes prepared in his speeches to ignore legality in favour of some purportedly higher principle which happened to support his point of view. But whatever his motives for appealing to Greek philosophical theories in order to denigrate his Roman political competitors, the effect was that he provided western Europe with a corpus of texts which has been used and re-used again and again in different times and circumstances. As none other than Julius Caesar is reported to have said of Cicero, he won a laurel wreath greater than any triumph, since his skills extended Rome's intellectual boundaries where others had only extended her territory:

> Omnium triumphorum laurea adepte maiorem, quanto plus est ingenii Romani terminos promovisse, quam imperii.
>
> (Pliny, NH 7, 117)

Suggestions for Further Study

1. One theme of this book is that while Cicero's writings, like any piece of literature, have had a life of their own during the 2,000 years since they were composed, they can also be understood *historically*, that is, as the products of a particular time and place in the past. Read any of Cicero's speeches and essays on rhetoric and philosophy, and consider what political motive Cicero may have had to 'publish' them. What did it mean in the first century BC to 'publish' a work? At what audience did Cicero direct such 'publications'?

2. Cicero considered his suppression of Catiline's conspiracy as his greatest achievement. Look at the different assessments by Sallust in his *Catiline* and by Cassius Dio (bk. 36, 43-4; 37, 29-42; 38, 12 and 18-29).

3. Consider the different skills and 'virtues' through which political success could be achieved in the late republic. What different backgrounds would politicians have needed in order to be able to demonstrate outstanding ability in: generalship; rhetoric; knowledge of the law; writing Latin poetry? How did the relevance of these skills to advancement in a political career change during the century from 140 to 40 BC? Did the Augustan principate lead to a decline in the importance attached to oratory, and a greater emphasis on law? [See e.g. Tacitus, *Dialogus*; W. Kunkel, *An Introduction to Roman Legal and Constitutional History* (1973).]

4. Consider the different skills and strategies exploited in their competition for political supremacy by Crassus, Pompey, Lucullus, Clodius, Caesar and Mark Antony. Were any of them really more successful than Cicero?

5. Would any of Rome's subjects in the province of Cilicia have considered Cicero a better-than-average governor?

6. Why and how did Cicero use the notion of 'Natural Law'? Where did he get the idea? How valid is it? How important was his analysis of it in the later history of European culture? [See e.g. A.P. d'Entrèves, *Natural Law* (London, 1951 etc.).]

7. Consider the different problems we are faced with when we use Cicero's speeches, his rhetorical or philosophical treatises, or his letters as sources for the political and cultural history of his age. In what respect can we ascribe objectivity to any of these categories of material?

Suggestions for Further Reading

An enormous amount of work has been done on the history of the late republic in recent years. The conclusions of work up to 1980 are summarised by M. Crawford in *Journal of Roman Studies* 71 (1981) 153-60. See also his Fontana paperback *The Roman Republic* (2nd edn, 1992); P.A. Brunt's essays on *The Fall of the Roman Republic* (1988); A.W. Lintott, *Violence in Republican Rome* (Oxford, 1968); T.P. Wiseman, *New Men in the Roman Senate 139 BC-AD 14* (Oxford, 1971) and (ed.) *Roman Political Life* (Exeter, 1985); Z. Yavetz, *Julius Caesar and his Public Image* (English version, London 1983). Many other books could be recommended.

Given the individualistic nature of late republican politics, it is not surprising that the period continues to be described through biographies of the participants. They include: M. Gelzer, *Caesar. Politician and Statesman* (English transl. P. Needham, 1969); A.M. Ward, *Marcus Crassus and the Late Roman Republic* (1977); A. Keaveney, *Sulla. The Last Republican* (1983) and *Lucullus* (1992); R. Seager, *Pompey* (Oxford, 1979); A. Roberts, *Mark Antony* (1988); and R.D. Weigel, *Lepidus* (1992).

There is no shortage of biographies of Cicero, chiefly as a politician. Among those which may be recommended are E. Rawson, *Cicero. A Portrait* (1975; repr. 1983: 308 pp. of text), C. Habicht, *Cicero the Politician* (1990: 99 pp. of text), and more substantially T.N. Mitchell's two volumes, *Cicero. The Ascending Years* (1979: 242 pp. text) and *Cicero. The Senior Statesman* (1991: 326 pp. text). Cicero's governorship of Cilicia is discussed in M. Wistrand, *Cicero Imperator* (Göteborg, 1979).

On Cicero's literary and philosophical work, one of the best introductions continues to be T.A. Dorey (ed.), *Cicero* (London, 1964). There is a *Greece & Rome* 'Survey' on *Cicero* by A.E. Douglas (1962). P. MacKendrick, *The Philosophical Books of Cicero* (London, 1989) contains summaries of the contents of the philosophical works and short discussions of major issues. There are still few better introductory surveys of Roman rhetoric than G. Kennedy, *The Art of Rhetoric in the*

Roman World (Princeton, 1972); for the speeches, P.M. MacKendrick, *The Speeches of Cicero: Context, Law, Rhetoric* (Duckworth, 1995); on characterisation in the speeches, see J.M. May, *Trials of Character. The Eloquence of Ciceronian Ethos* (Chapel Hill/London, 1988). Discussions of individual works normally require knowledge of Latin and are sometimes difficult, but may be rewarding; see e.g. A.E. Douglas' edition of *Cicero. Brutus* (Oxford, 1966), R.G.M. Nisbet's *Cicero, in Pisonem* (Oxford, 1961), or M.T. Griffin and E.M. Atkins, *On Duties* (Cambridge, 1991). For the relationship between the text of a speech and its performance, see R.G.M. Nisbet, 'The Orator and the Reader: Manipulation and response in Cicero's *Fifth Verrine*', in A.J. Woodman and J. Powell (eds), *Author and Audience in Latin Literature* (Cambridge, 1992). B.W. Frier, *The Rise of the Roman Jurists* (Princeton, 1985), elucidates not just the *Pro Caecina* but the general confusion of Roman law in the late republic. On the letters, see D.R. Shackleton-Bailey, *Cicero's Letters to Atticus* (Cambridge 1965-70) and *Cicero. Epistulae ad Familiares* (Cambridge, 1977).

Naturally interest in Cicero is not confined only to English-language scholars. Especially on Nachleben, there is little in English to compare with Th. Zielinski's *Cicero im Wandel der Jahrhunderte* (Leipzig, 1912).

On the general cultural background of first-century Italy, see E. Rawson, *Intellectual Life in the Late Roman Republic* (London, 1985); for the previous century, E.S. Gruen, *Culture and National Identity in Republican Rome* (London, 1993). D.C. Earl, *The Moral and Political Tradition of Rome* (London, 1967) is still relevant.

Easily available translations of the sources for the period:

A) Cicero's works available in Penguin Classics:
Cicero. Selected Works, transl. M. Grant (1960): contains Against Verres I; 23 letters; Philippic II; On Duties III: and On Old Age.
Cicero. The Nature of the Gods, transl. H.C.P. McGregor, with introduction by J.M. Ross (1972).
Cicero. Selected Political Speeches, transl. M.Grant (1969): contains On the Command of Gnaeus Pompeius; Against Catiline I-IV; In Defence of Archias; In Defence of Caelius Rufus; In Defence of Milo; In Support of Marcellus; and Philippic I.
Cicero. On the Good Life, transl. M. Grant (1971): contains Tusculan V, On Duties II, Laelius on Friendship, On the Orator I, and the Dream of Scipio.

B) Greek and Roman histories and biographies of the period:
I. Scott-Kilvert, *Plutarch: Fall of the Roman Republic* (1958: includes the life of Cicero) and *Makers of Rome* (1965).
Plutarch, *Life of Cicero*, ed. and transl. J.L. Moles (Aris & Philips, 1988), which may be read with the commentary by M.J. Edwards, *Plutarch: The Lives of Pompey, Caesar and Cicero* (Companion to the Penguin Translation, BCP, 1991).

Histories of the period by Cassius Dio and Appian are available in the Loeb Classical Library; Caesar, Sallust and Suetonius are in Penguin Classics. Volume I of N. Lewis and M. Reinhold, *Roman Civilisation* (2nd edn, New York, 1966) is a useful collection of important extracts relating to the period.

Fig. 19 The census of 70 BC, from the so-called 'Altar of Domitius Ahenobarbus' in the Louvre, Paris. In the centre, the censor L. Gellius Poplicola offers sacrifice; to the right are the three animals (*suovetaurilia*) sacrificed to purify the Roman people in the *lustrum*. On the left, the censors' officials compile the list of citizens: two of them are shown reporting in military dress, to be assigned to their 'centuries' (electoral units in the centuriate assembly).

Some Technical Terms

aedilis (aedile): Junior magistrate responsible for public buildings (*aedes*) and places, hence for ensuring that market prices e.g. for corn were fair; and with responsibility for putting on various public festivals.

amicitia, amicus ('friendship', 'friend'): At Rome, as in many societies, friendship is a formal social institution. A man has the obligation to help his friends, and to listen to their advice. *Amicitiae* therefore include political associations, but that does not exclude 'friendship' in our sense: see P.A. Brunt, *The Fall of the Roman Republic* (Oxford, 1988) ch. 7.

census (censorship): Originally perhaps a ritual cleansing of the Roman people, in the republic it involved updating the list of citizens liable to military service (and with the right to vote). The censors decided to which electoral unit and status-group to assign each citizen; this included deciding who was to be a senator. A census normally took place every five years (a *lustrum*: see illustration opposite).

comitia: Assemblies of (a) the Roman people, drawn up by military units (centuries, hence *comitia centuriata*) to elect magistrates and pass laws (*leges*), and (b) the plebeians, drawn up by tribes (hence *comitia tributa*) to pass *plebiscita* which had the force of law.

consilium: The semi-formal group of *amici* whose advice on important issues a Roman was bound to take. The Senate fulfilled this function for magistrates.

consul (abbr. 'cos.'): The pair of magistrates who, under the republic, held supreme power. The *consules ordinarii* gave their names to the year in which they held office. If a consul died, a 'suffect' was elected in his place. A former consul was known as a 'consular' (*consularis*).

contio: A semi-formal assembly of Roman citizens called by a magistrate in order to make an important announcement.

dictator: An extraordinary magistrate, appointed in the early republic to take supreme command of the army in time of crisis. By the mid-republic, *dictatores* were appointed only to hold elections in the absence of the consuls. Sulla and Caesar used the office to give legitimacy to their seizure of power.

91

equites (equestrian order): Formally, the cavalry arm of the Roman army; in practice, the term was applied to all wealthy land-owning citizens ('gentry', we might say) who were not members of the Senate.

imperium: The constitutional right, granted by election or by an extraordinary vote of the Roman people, to command in war; it was held by consuls and praetors. The commander was an *imperator*.

legate: Provincial governors and other military commanders would select (hence *legati*) experienced friends to help them during their period of office.

pomerium: The ritual boundary of the city of Rome.

pontifex: One of the groups conventionally called 'priests'. The *pontifices* advised magistrates on matters of religious law. Their president, the *Pontifex Maximus*, effectively controlled the exercise of state religion.

praetor: The second most senior annual magistracy. The main function of the praetors was administering justice.

provincia: The 'sphere of action' of a Roman magistrate. Thus the Urban Praetor (*praetor urbanus*) was responsible for lawsuits between Roman citizens, the Peregrine Praetor (*praetor peregrinus*) for lawsuits between Romans and non-citizens (*peregrini*). When the Romans had to rule overseas territories (Sicily and Sardinia from 238 BC), these territories became permanent *provinciae*. Cicero's *provincia* of Cilicia in fact included responsibility for much of Anatolia, as well as Cyprus.

quaestor: A junior magistrate, normally in his early thirties, who would assist magistrates with *imperium* in matters of administration (especially finance).

Senate, senator: The supreme council at Rome, whose collective advice was authoritative for magistrates, although it did not have the force of law. Thus the *Senatus consultum ultimum* (SCU, 'Last decree') of 63 BC advised Cicero and the other magistrates to take action to protect the republic from Catiline, but did not have the force to set aside laws protecting Roman citizens from execution without trial. Ex-magistrates were normally senators for the rest of their lives, unless they were expelled as unworthy at a *census*.

tribunes: Each year, the plebeian assembly (*comitia tributa*, consisting of electoral units called 'tribes': there were 35 in the late republic) elected ten tribunes whose task had originally been to protect the interests of the plebeians against magistrates. While they continued to have that function in the late republic, their special powers also made them potential political opponents both of individual magistrates and of the authority of the Senate.